APPALACHIAN DREAMER

Dick McVey
www.dickmcvey.com

DEDICATION

This book is dedicated to my sister Frances (Pud) McVey Stacy. If it wasn't for her, I could not have had the life I dreamed about. She sacrificed many things for me as you will see in the book and, in our mother's final years on earth, she moved in with her and took care of her daily needs. That allowed me to travel all around the world playing music.

FOREWARD

Dick McVey is a true Renaissance Man. I have known him for decades and he never fails to surprise me when he shares stories about the journey of his life.

Starting from humble beginnings in Southern West Virginia to becoming one of the key players in the Nashville music scene, Dick was one of the few industry professionals who knew how to adapt to the times, reinvent himself and take advantage of opportunities that others didn't have the skills to see.

For those who want a career in the music business, Dick gives you a glimpse into the inner workings of an industry that is generally closed to outsiders.

My career as an entertainment lawyer has led me to understand that this type of behavior is not unique to the music business and Dick's life experiences offer a pathway for success in whatever career you may choose to embrace.

In telling his story, Dick doesn't sugarcoat anything. It's what stands Dick apart from 99% of the music industry. He offers us the good and bad; the pretty and the ugly; the bright lights and glory; and the dark and dirty of his life. He holds nothing back and through his sharing, we come to embrace a man who is a true survivor.

This is one of those books that you can pick up, read a chapter and put it down for another day, yet it's compelling enough to hold your attention until you read it through.

At the end of this read, you will feel happy. You will feel complete. And you will feel the joy of knowing Dick McVey. Enjoy the read and the journey.

Wayne Halper

ABOUT WAYNE HALPER

Wayne Halper has been an entertainment lawyer since 1979. In addition to counseling and managing many artists, he served as Senior VP of Business Affairs at Capitol Records (Garth Brooks, Tanya Tucker), General Manager/ Head of Label Operations for DreamWorks Records (Toby Keith, Randy Travis) and Treasurer for the Country Music Association, the Country Music Hall of Fame and NARAS (the Grammy organization). In 2003, Halper was designated as Father of the Year in Nashville, Tennessee (his proudest achievement).

CONTENTS:

CONTENTS (cont):

CHAPTER 1: DREAMING BIG

It's showtime! I stand up in the dressing room and strap on my guitar. The crowd is buzzing and an occasional yell and whistle ring out. My heart is pumping. I'm feeling an adrenaline rush. Crewmembers greet me in the hallway with flashlights to direct me to the stage. Police officers are stationed along the path, just in case. Arriving at the side of the stage, the stage crew wishes me luck. Suddenly, there I am. There are thousands of screaming fans applauding and yelling as I walk on the huge stage. The drummer counts off the first song, the crowd goes wild, and my adrenaline kicks into overdrive. The sound and energy of the band is driving me as the lights, effects and fog envelope the stage. There is an indescribable energy that surrounds me. I am living the dream. And then…. then, I'd wake up.

This was a recurring dream I had for years, and if you're a musician or singer I bet you've had that same dream. The actual wake-up always gave me a kind of sick feeling in the pit of my stomach. I would think to myself, "That would be incredible, but it will never happen." But then it did!

I grew up in southern West Virginia in the heart of America's coalfields, and, in that area known as Appalachia, dreams were rarely more than that—just dreams. When I would mention my dream to people, most would scoff and tell me I was foolish to believe I could ever have that kind of success or even make a living as a musician. Unfortunately, doubters exist all around the world. They discourage many talented people from ever following their dreams. The general life plan for most people where I grew up was to get through school, get a job, get married, have kids, and work and live until you died. Many never venture beyond state lines and for some, never go too far beyond the county where they were born. Don't get me wrong, there's nothing wrong with that life plan. That is, unless you are someone like me who wanted to see the world and experience things I saw on TV, in movies, and in my dreams.

I was born and raised in Pemberton, West Virginia, a small town near Beckley. I had a great family. My Dad (Richard) was a surveyor and engineer who mapped out the workings of coal mines and drew maps showing the progress of the mining. Above ground, he also surveyed land and property, but his primary job was working for coal companies. He worked hard and was well respected by his bosses, co-workers and friends. It was commonplace for people to say to me, "Your Dad is a good man." That always made me smile and I strived to have that same type of reputation. I was proud of him and, even at a young age, appreciated his hard work.

Dad would come home from the mines, face black with coal dust, but he always had time to spend with me. He taught me a lot about baseball. He was known locally as a good player and played for several local teams. He spent hours playing baseball with me and taught me that practice makes you better. I think it was his dream for me to play professional baseball, although he never said that or encouraged me to dream that big.

My Mom (Dorothy or "Dot," as people called her) was a wonderful homemaker and mother. I was so blessed to have her as "mom". My sister (Frances), or "Pud" as we called her, was nine years older than me and the victim of lots of "little brother" pranks and abuse. I was a wrestling fan and Pud would often be my unwilling opponent. I don't think I ever hurt her too bad. But I did get a whipping one time for dragging her across the floor by her hair, a tactic I'd seen used by wrestlers on TV and assumed it was proper wrestling protocol.

I attended local public schools. Pemberton Elementary School, Coal City Elementary School, Stoco Junior High School, Stoco High School and later Mullens High School, where I graduated in 1966.

I never really thought of us as being poor. Compared to most of my friends and classmates, we seemed to be pretty well off. We had pinto beans and fried potatoes almost every day with

meat added on the weekends. We went to the A&P Grocery Store in Beckley on payday Fridays where we would get hamburger meat and a roast or chicken for the weekend. And then on Monday it was back to pinto beans and skillet fried potatoes with onions. My Dad loved it and strangely enough I still love that meal today.

We usually had a garden, which I hated because of the weeding and hoeing. However, I sure enjoyed those home-grown tomatoes and fresh corn on the cob. During the summers there were always fresh vegetables. Mom canned (preserved) a lot of the vegetables and fruits for us to use throughout the winter months. Eating out was extremely rare. Movies were even rarer and trips to Beckley were usually for a doctor's visit or getting a tooth pulled. As crazy as it seems, it was so exciting to go to Beckley that I would endure the dentist or a doctor's visit in order to go to G.C. Murphy's Department store for lunch and to get a toy—not toys. One particular trip to the doctor was because I enjoyed eating rotten wood and coal. My Mom was very concerned about it, but the doctor simply said, "Let him eat it. It won't hurt him." Old time medical advice at its best.

Beckley was a typical town in the '50s and '60s. At Christmas time it was magical with the all the department stores, Christmas decorations on the streets, Santa Claus at Grant Department store (I was scared of him), people scurrying about and even more special if there was snow. Dad was notorious for his last-minute Christmas Eve shopping, a trait he passed on to me.

I can still hear the old washing machine swishing water around and Mom hanging our clothes out to dry when they were done. I also remember her yelling at us if we played too close to clothesline because we had knocked the prop pole out a few times sending the clothes to ground. We had an Electrolux vacuum cleaner (on skids – not wheels) that had a wonderful droning sound that put me to sleep on the couch many Saturday mornings. We had a dial up phone and we were on a "party line" where we could eavesdrop or listen in on our neighbors' phone calls. The dogs lived out-doors, ate table scraps, and it was rare they ever went to the vet.

Most entertainment was self-made. Usually, I was play-ing in the woods, finding a

grapevine to cut and swing on, playing sports, and hanging out with my buddies Kenneth and Keith Lester. We had fun and I'd often get in trouble if I ventured too far away from home, espe-cially if I got caught going near Piney Creek. Mom could whis-tle by cupping her hands and that was my signal to come home. If I was too far away and couldn't hear that distinct sound, I was in trouble.

The highlight of winter was sledding. We had a great hill that would occasionally carry your sled (and you) through a barbed-wire fence, into a tree or over the hill dumping you in the road. Sometimes you'd slam into someone trying to climb back up the hill. There were more than a few mishaps. We'd stay outside until we couldn't feel our fingers. Often come home covered in black soot from burning an old tire to warm us up be-tween sledding runs. There's no doubt we probably got frostbite a time or two, but nothing that washing your hands in hot water wouldn't fix. It was a wonderful time to be alive and to grow up in those mountains with a great family surrounding you.

CHAPTER 2: MY MUSICAL JOURNEY BEGINS

Our family was musically inclined. Both my grandfathers and several uncles played instruments. Mom, Dad and my uncle Remus McVey had a gospel trio, and they practiced a lot at our house. My Dad played guitar and I would always hang around during their rehearsals. That peaked my first interest in playing the guitar. My uncle Hester McVey played autoharp and banjo and occasionally he and my Dad would get together for jam sessions. Both Hester and Remus were instrumental in encouraging me to pursue my music.

When I was around 10 years old, I asked my Dad to teach me to play guitar. He showed me three chords – G, C, and D. He told me if I learned those chords, I would be able to play a lot of different songs. I learned the chords, but it was hard. I couldn't make the chord changes fast enough to play a song that wasn't disrupted with all sorts of stalls and stops. It would take me three minutes to play a two-minute song. That's when I realized playing the guitar this wasn't as easy as I thought. So, I opted to spend that practice time playing sports instead.

In late 1963, my Dad was promoted to the job of Superintendent of Mining Operations for Amigo Smokeless Coal Company, the company where he had been employed as an engineer for a number of years. The promotion also meant he had to live on-site, and we would be relocating to a coal camp in Amigo, West Virginia. It was only 15 miles from Pemberton, but it took 30 minutes to make the drive because of the winding mountain highway. That seemed like forever back then. I was in the 10th grade at Stoco High School in Coal City, West Virginia, and the news of the move devastated me. All the friends I had grown up with, including the Lester boys, were not going to be part of my life any longer. The move also meant I had to transfer to Mullens High School in Mullens and start over with people I didn't know. I was not happy.

I met my first wife, Judi Smith, in Junior High School and was enamored with her. She was a majorette in the band and, to me, the most beautiful girl in school. The only problem was, she had a boyfriend and simply wasn't interested in me. We rode the same bus home, so I was always trying to sit near her. Her boyfriend got off the bus before Judi and me, so I always tried to talk to her after he would get off. Our move meant that I would lose any chance of seeing her. At 14 that was quite a heartbreak, even though it was a one-sided relationship. After we moved, she was only 15 miles away, but it seemed more like 100 miles. I would never get the opportunity to win her heart. She was popular and I didn't have much to offer.

The new house in Amigo was much bigger than our previous house and there was a full-unfinished basement that was big enough for me to ride my bicycle in the winter. There was an upstairs that was big as well. Dad bought a pool table and a dartboard, and the upstairs became our rec room. I was trying to learn to ride a skateboard and there was room there to do that.

The most important thing in the rec room was my record player. I enjoyed listening to records in the background while taking advantage of the other entertainment options.

Across the street from the house was a gas station and store, and that became an excellent incentive for me to live there. Soda pop, candy and ice cream only 40 feet away, and a pin ball machine to top it all off. Less than 100 yards down the road was the "Red Bird," a trolley car style restaurant where you get a burger and shake, and next to that was a full-size baseball field complete with grandstands. The carnival came through once a year and set up in the ball field. I started thinking, "This may not be so bad after all."

Larry McKinney lived across the street with his grandfather in the gas station. He was my age, an outgoing guy, and we met the first day I moved in. On the first day I went to the new high school, he sat with me on the bus and took me to the principal's office to get signed in when we arrived. Principal Lewis D'Antoni was a nice man. He told Larry to look after me at the end of the day to make sure I got on the right school bus to go home. Larry assured Mr. D'Antoni he would do that, but at the end of the day, Larry never showed up and I missed the bus.

I went to Principal D'Antoni's office and called home. My Dad was at work and my sister, who was a schoolteacher, wouldn't be home for another hour. Principal D'Antoni took me to his house, about a half-mile from the high school and treated me like family. He was a legend in Mullens since he had a successful career as the high school basketball coach. His son, Danny, who was two years ahead of me in school, later became the coach of the Marshall Thundering Herd basketball team. His other son Mike, who was two years behind me in school, became an award-winning NBA coach.

I never forgot the way they treated me. I thought if this is the way people treat you here, then this is going to be OK.

The transition to a new high school wasn't as smooth as I had hoped. I found out the "city kids" who lived in Mullens kind of looked down on "kids from a coal camp." It wasn't bad but there were some kids who "tested me." Some of those people eventually became my friends once they got to know me. There were some uncomfortable times in the early days at school, but it all smoothed out over time.

I had been an all-star baseball player growing up and after six seasons in Little League and Senior League, my batting average was just under .500. I went to a pro tryout where there were scouts from the Pittsburgh Pirates and Cincinnati Reds. I was encouraged that told me they would like to talk to me when I got through college. That really pumped me up and gave me confidence that I might just have a chance at making it as a pro baseball player. I knew I was a good player, but then I got a life lesson. When I tried out for the high school baseball team, I didn't make the team. I had a great tryout and actually hit some home runs. That was tremendously disappointing for my Dad, and me but it taught me about "politics" and how life isn't always fair, even at the high school level. I was bitter about it. Fortunately, something came along that made me forget it happened.

CHAPTER 3: THE FIRST BAND

It was Sunday, February 9, 1964, and my life's focus turned from baseball to music. The Beatles appeared on the Ed Sullivan Show, and I remember my Dad asking me before the show, "Who are these Beatles?" After the show it was evident my parents were not fans of the longhaired quartet. When I told Dad I wanted to let my hair grow out, he promised me that wouldn't happen as long as I lived under his roof.

The show that night changed my life and me. As I sat watching the TV, I realized The Beatles were living my dream and had turned it into reality. As I sat there in that coal camp in West Virginia, The Beatles gave me hope that someday my dream could become a reality too. My drive to practice and perform was greatly enhanced. I can't stress enough how the boys from Liverpool impacted me. I bought the records, I watched the live performances and I saw the effect they had on girls and, at 14, I was starting to see girls in a different way.

There was no doubt The Beatles influenced and stimulated thousands of young people to become musicians. It also pushed those that were already musicians to put together bands. In one instance, some of my high school classmates (Mark Akers, David Runion, Bob Hearn and Rex McCoy) put together a band called "The Born Losers". Shortly after The Beatles appeared on the Ed Sullivan Show, "The Born Losers" played a school assembly and did the Beatles song, "I Feel Fine." Mark Akers was the lead guitarist and Mark nailed the sound and the guitar lick on the intro of that song - I remember it vividly and can still hear it in my head today. As soon as he kicked off that song, the girls started screaming and swooning and that's all it took. I had seen enough - I was hooked. I had to learn to play guitar and have a band.

My Dad had a couple of guitars, but they weren't "cool enough" for me to play. He made a deal with me that if I learned

to play the "uncool" guitars he would buy me a "cool" one. I talked him into buying me an official electric Silvertone guitar from Sears. I remember my disappointment when that guitar seemed to be forever on back order, and I was stuck playing his old Gibson. Little did I know the value of that guitar. The delivery truck to our local Sears store ran once a week so it would kill me when my Mom would call Sears and get that "not yet" answer. I can't describe to you how excited I was when we finally picked it up. Now I could look and sound like a real rock and roll guitar player - at least that's what I told myself.

I was driven to learn to play as quickly as I could so I could put together my own band, however I also remembered my first attempt at learning guitar and how much hard work was going to be involved. I also found that some of The Beatles' songs were not written using those basic simple chords my Dad taught me. I was going to have to expand my three-chord knowledge and learn, not only how to contort my fingers to make those new chords, but how to make them sound as pristine as George Harrison did.

I always thought people were exaggerating when they would say "I practiced till my fingers bled," but I can tell you, I practiced until my fingers bled. I bought chord books so I could learn more. There were no You Tube videos, or instructional videos during that time, so I taught myself the best I could. I practiced most every minute of every day when I was home. I was obsessed, I couldn't play enough. My friends rarely saw me and even though the ends of my fingers looked like bloody stubs, I continued to play through the pain. I wanted this bad.

I wish I had been able to take lessons or learn from a professional musician. A Beatles chord book was my constant companion, and even though the chord diagrams were in the book, some of them were hard for me to figure out on my own. As a result of having limited resources and lack of a real professional training, I taught myself some really bad playing habits that still haunt me to this day.

As I progressed, the thought of trying to put a band together started taking shape. I began asking around school if anyone knew any musicians, and somebody mentioned the names Brian Wilcox, another guitar player and Dean Morgan, a bass player. Over the next few days, I spoke with them and one Saturday we all got together at my house. At the time I was playing, what I interpreted to be, lead guitar. Looking back, it wasn't that at all, and to be honest, I wasn't very good, but I was determined. I basically had one or two signature licks that would work on a lot of the simpler songs, but The Beatles' songs required a lot of time to get the signature licks of their songs.

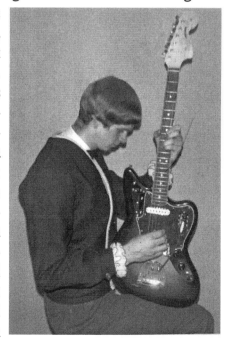

My goal of playing music was slowly becoming a reality, but my goal of having girls talk to me was still not happening. Fortunately, one of Brian's neighbors was a pretty red-headed girl named Brenda Way-caster and, when I asked Brian about her, he told me she didn't have a boyfriend. I got up the courage to talk to her and eventually we called ourselves a couple. There were two advantages to seeing Brenda - I could catch a bus to go see her and I could tell my parents Brian and I were working on music as an excuse.

When I wasn't seeing Brenda or going to school, I continued to practice and started organizing a band. My Dad had bought an old marching band snare drum and at one practice, my friend Brian Smith came over and played the snare drum and sang some songs with us. After that rehearsal, we knew we needed a drummer with a full drum kit to fill out the band. I had come up with the name "The Offbeats" for the band and, while it was fitting, the guys didn't like it and vetoed that name.

I got the Dictionary (remember there is no Google) and I started looking up musical terms and I found the word, "Rondeau" which was defined as a form of medieval Renaissance French poetry and music. I thought it was perfect for a couple of reasons. For one, it was a musical term and second, it was unlikely that any other band would ever use that name. The only downside was the spelling and pronunciation, but it was unique and unusual, and the guys liked it.

At this point, our biggest problem is we don't have a drummer and I couldn't get any of the drummers at our high school interested in playing with us. I don't think the thought of driving 10 miles to a coal camp to practice appealed to them. I remembered a guy named Freddy Crowson at my old high school who played drums and when I got in touch with him, he agreed to give it a shot. He had a nice drum kit, but, best of all, he had a car and could drive. We had everything we needed except stage experience and gigs. We all wanted to do this, so we worked hard to be a band, and it slowly started coming together. I know we drove my Mom nuts, and, while she was encouraging, she also asked us to practice outside on the front porch. I'm sure that gave her some relief, but I'm also sure it annoyed the neighbors; however, I don't ever remember getting a complaint.

One evening as we practiced a car pulled up in front of the house and stopped. After a couple of songs, a young man came up and introduced himself as Squire Parsons. He would later gain worldwide notoriety for writing and singing the hit Gospel song "Beulah Land." He was about our age at the time and living near Charleston.

We were all growing up in an area where there wasn't a lot of money, so buying musical instruments wasn't very high on our parent's priority list. We were playing entry-level instruments through cheap amplifiers. It was so bad that Dean had taken a standard six-string electric guitar and turned it into a four-string bass guitar. Oddly enough it worked, but that was just one example of the equipment problems we faced and had to solve as a band. Our parents were not convinced of our dedication to being rock stars, so they were hesitant at first to invest in any high dollar guitars and amplifiers. Looking back, it probably made sense because they didn't realize how much time, we had invested in being a real band.

In 1965 I got a Sears a Silvertone tube guitar amplifier (model 1484 / 60 watts for you gear enthusiasts). For its time it was a huge amplifier. It had two 12" speakers and a piggyback style that made it look even bigger. It had four input channels so we could plug in our guitar and microphone. It had a built-in reverb that sounded like thunder it you accidentally bumped it. This amp was $150 but it was a "must have" and we told our parents we had to have it. Sears also made a bass version of the same amp so, in the end, we all had a matched set of amplifiers on stage.

The Silvertone guitar was serving me well, but I had seen and played a Fender Jaguar guitar at Jan Campbell Music in Beckley and it played so well and was so easy on my fingers that I loved it. It was so expensive that I wouldn't ask my parents to buy it, but then something happened. The salesman asked, "Do you have anything you could trade?" My Dad had bought my sister a beautiful Wurlitzer upright piano from them a few years before and I blurted out "We have a piano you sold us!" I thought my sister was going to pass out. He got the paperwork for the piano and he came back with an offer to trade us even for the guitar. I looked at my sister and realized the deal was probably not going to happen. I knew I had a lot of work ahead of me to persuade her to give up that piano. I never gave one thought about the value of the piano at the time but looking back it was probably worth more than that guitar. All I knew at the time was I wanted that guitar and here was a chance to get it - if I could get my sister to agree.

That following week I gave her my best sales pitch, "You rarely play it, and the stool is just a place to lay your coat when you came in the door." After much debate, she agreed to let me trade the piano and I got a guitar that was so much better than the Silvertone. Brian also got a new guitar and a Vox amplifier, a smaller version of one like The Beatles used. Dean continued to play the guitar converted to bass. We didn't care because he was a great musician and it actually sounded good.

One of our biggest issues was that we didn't understand the concept of harmony and how to sing harmony parts. We were doing a lot of songs by the British bands where the singers, especially The Beatles, were harmonizing with one another. When we sang together, we couldn't understand why it didn't sound the same. We were singing in unison with each other, while they were singing harmony parts with one another. It took a while to figure things out and I don't think we ever did get it right until near the end. As my ear developed, I was able to figure out harmony parts, but I often chuckle to myself when I think about our ignorance at that time.

We practiced and we thought we were sounding pretty good, so I started to try and find a place to play our first gig. My sister came through for me again. She was teaching at Mark Twain Junior High School and they were going to have a dance. She asked if we wanted to play and we were excited to take this show off the front porch to an actual stage. Needless to say, we jumped at that opportunity and it started the beginning of my professional career at age 15. I think we made like $12 each. It was a great start for the band, but I found out that while the girls really liked us, the boys didn't care for us so much.

Following that first gig, we were all driven to play as often as we could, and I started pushing hard to get us more jobs. I didn't realize it at the time, but I was getting an education in the music business. The drive to play and sing was also the driving force in finding gigs.

After that first gig, I became an agent, a manager, an accountant, a publicity person and so on. To me it was fun and challenging and to this day I've never considered it work. I decided I would play at every opportunity I could get, so I got some business cards made up and I started inquiring at local schools and teen clubs.

I set short-term achievable goals and, as things progressed, the goals kept getting bigger and harder to achieve but I never saw anything as unachievable. My efforts were paying off and it seemed we were staying busy for a start-up band. Remember, back then there were no computers, no fax machines, no Internet, or cell phones. The two methods of communication were the telephone and the U.S. Mail.

I sent out more than one hundred letters and made lots of telephone calls to anybody I thought might hire us. We were too young to play at clubs, so my focus was playing other high schools and teen clubs in Raleigh and Wyoming counties. Oceana High School, a rival school 26 miles down the road from Mullens decided they were going to hold dances in the band room after home football games. Thomas Goheen, who was the band director at the school used the money to raise funds for the high school band and we became his "go to" band for those dances. The dances were a lot of fun, and Mr. Goheen looked out for us, since the Oceana boys weren't thrilled about us Mullens guys singing to their girls. And as Freddy would say if there was any friction, "Hey, I'm not from Mullens."

Freddy was attending Stoco High School and he was friends with my first love Judi Smith. Freddy got us a gig at Stoco, and when we played, low and behold, there she was in all her beauty. She is now looking at me a little differently because I'm in a band, so I got up my nerve and asked for her phone number. That doesn't solve the problem that she is still 15 miles away, I can't drive yet, she still has a boyfriend, and back then it was a long-distance call from Amigo to Coal City, even though it was nearby. Judi and my cousin Peggy were both majorettes and Peggy helped me with getting my foot in the door.

I couldn't run up my parents' phone bill, so I would call her from the pay phone across the road from our house. I would save my quarters and call her for a few minutes every day. I was telling a friend at school about it costing me a lot of money to call and he showed me how I could grind down a penny that would fit in the dime slot of the pay phone. My Dad had a grinder in the basement, so I spent a lot of time grinding down pennies. I don't remember what I told my parents I was doing, but I assure you they would not have liked the idea that I was defrauding the phone company. I hate to think what they would have done to me if I had gotten caught.

Freddy had a 1959 Ford Galaxy. It was a two-toned yellow and white beauty and best of all we could get all our equipment in the trunk. It was huge. We didn't have a P.A. system since we were singing through the amps, and we learned how to use every inch of space in that car. The packing lessons I learned back then have been part of my life skills ever since.

The trips to and from Oceana to play on Friday nights were always interesting. The roads were winding and narrow and often my sister would drive and chaperone us. My parent's biggest fear was having a car wreck. Driving home late at night and knowing there were drunks on the road kept them up waiting on us many nights. One night on our way home a car passed us and was driving erratically. West Virginia roads are challenging enough if you're sober, and it wasn't long before the car ran up the side of the mountain and flipped over on its top right in front of us. It was a man and woman. She had been tossed into the back seat and then to the roof of the car, which is now upside down. She was screaming at the top of her lungs that her leg was broken. Freddy got to the car first and was trying to calm her down. The man was walking around cussing and telling her to shut up. I could hear Brian and Dean arguing and when I looked over, they were fighting over the flashlight to see who was going to direct traffic. We stayed until other people arrived and got out of there before the police arrived. It was already late, and my sister wanted to get us home.

On another trip to Oceana, it had snowed and, while the

roads had been cleared, there were occasional big clumps of snow and ice that had been jarred loose from under the fenders of vehicles. We thought it would be fun to hit them with the car and smash them and we had done a couple successfully. We could see a big one coming up in front of us and we implored Freddy to speed up and bust it up. It wasn't snow or ice, but a big rock. As soon as we hit it the car started making an awful racket and the oil pressure went to zero. We had busted the oil pan. We were in sight of the place we were playing so we got the car to someone's yard and they helped us haul the equipment to the gig. I think my sister came and picked us up and the next morning my Dad, Freddy and I went down and got it fixed. It was a big blow to our expenses and embarrassing. I don't think we ever told anyone we hit that rock on purpose.

In Sophia, West Virginia there was a Teen Town on Main Street and we were playing there regularly and drawing good crowds. A man named Tony Milano, who also ran the supermarket in Sophia, operated teen Town. He took a lot of  interest in us as a band and believed if we would put out a record, it would help his business and if it became a hit, we would all be rich. It wasn't unusual for young bands to reach the top of the charts in those days, and so a delusional Mr. Milano put up the money for us to go to Magna Recording Studio in Beckley to do our first single. I don't want you to think Mr. Milano was the only person who was delusional in all this - we all had stardom and dollar signs floating in our minds.

Our original plan was to do two cover songs that we had been playing out live, but then Mr. Milano said he wanted us to do something we had written. The problem was we hadn't written anything. It was a few days before the session, so I got my guitar and wrote a song called "Anymore". It was the story of a young man in love but the girl in the song has dumped him and she doesn't love him "anymore". It was the only song I've ever written by myself and when I listen to it today, it reinforces the reason why I never wrote another song.

The record was a 45-rpm with two sides. "Anymore" was on one side and the flip side was a cover of The Beatles song, "Day Tripper." That song had a really cool signature guitar lick that I played incorrectly. It haunts me to this day and if you have ever done something wrong on a record, you will hear it every time you listen to it. In addition to that, my vocal sounded nasally, and our unison "harmonies" were just awful. The icing on the cake came when we finally got the records from the pressing plant, and they had misspelled our name as "Rondeus" instead of "Rondeaus".

As I learned more about the music business, I found out the guy who owned the studio published my song without my permission. I'm not sure that, since I was a minor, Mr. Milano unintentionally signed my rights away. A lesson learned, but years after it happened.

We were excited about the recording project to say the least. We thought we were ready to be in a recording studio, but we were not. The engineer at the studio was trying to help us as much as he could. We are on the clock and Mr. Milano, who is paying by the hour kept looking at his watch. Recording is rarely a fast process and, when you add to that a rookie band in the studio for the first time, it makes for a long night.

Russ Hicks, who later made a name for himself in Nashville as a great steel guitarist, was there, and with him being a local hero we were all intimidated that "the man" himself was present to watch our session. I'm sure he had a giggle or two.

Long story short, we were very proud of the recording, we sold a few and some of the brave local DJ's actually gave us a spin or two. The newspaper did a nice article on us, so we were local hot shots for a while. The stardom never came, Mr. Milano ran his grocery store and most of the records ended up under our beds at home.

Oddly enough the West Virginia Music Hall Of Fame features

us in a You Tube video performing "Anymore." The Hall Of Fame also has an archive of information and material on the band. The band was also featured in a book about garage bands in the 60s.

As is the case with most bands, life often gets in the way and when I graduated from high school, I realized my bandmates would soon be off to college and we would be too far apart to keep the band together. So that, coupled with the demands of college, dealt me my first setback with the breakup of my first band.

CHAPTER 4: COLLEGE DAYS

I went to Concord College in Athens, West Virginia, in the Fall of 1966. We jokingly called it UCLA (University of Concord Located in Athens). It was my first time away from home. Since my parents had protected me a lot from the real world, it was a disaster. My sister had attended this college and graduated, so I think they felt that same plan would work for me. It did not.

The first thing I learned in college was that it was not mandatory to go to class. The second thing I learned was that I could come and go as I pleased and stay out as late as I wanted. I stayed in trouble a lot and only lasted two semesters. One reason for my bad start was a friend of mine named Delmar Lawson. Delmar had won a new Mustang in a contest sponsored by Amoco gas company. Delmar brought his car to college, which was against the rules since freshmen weren't allowed to have a car on campus. Technically, according to Delmar, he wasn't parking the car on campus, so he convinced himself and me that it was alright. I also had a Mustang, so I reported this information to my Dad, and he reluctantly agreed to let me take my car as long as I didn't park it on campus and would only drive it back and forth between home and school. Bending to peer pressure, I was hauling friends here and there and, if my Dad had checked the mileage, the car would have never left our home.

An example of my irresponsibility was Delmar and I drag racing right through the middle of campus. The campus police stopped us, and we had to have a little meeting with the Dean. I was scared to death as we reported to the office because I knew if this got back to my Dad, I wouldn't be able to keep the car at school. Delmar was a little more laid back about it all and since he didn't want to be in college, his attitude was much more indifferent than mine.

The Dean came into the office and asked if we knew about the "no car on campus for freshmen" rule and we both agreed we did. At that point Delmar starts to lay out our defense, which didn't hold water since we were caught on campus even though we parked elsewhere. I kept my mouth shut, but Delmar continued to argue with the Dean. The Dean read the rule to us and dished out our punishment. We were on "Social Probation" for the rest of the year. That meant we couldn't attend any social function at the school, other than attending classes and eating in the cafeteria.

At this point I breathed a sigh of relief. But just as I got up to leave, Delmar jumped up and proclaimed, "This school is run by a bunch of Mickey Mouse rules and I'm tired of being a Mouseketeer." My mouth dropped and Delmar stormed out of the office. I exited in more of civilized manner, but I wasn't sure if Delmar's actions might stimulate further repercussions. Thank God, it did not and my parents were not notified.

I didn't learn a lesson from that and shortly after some friends talked me into climbing the water tower with them. I'm not afraid of heights, but the ladder to the water tower was on an angle going up until the last 20 feet when the ladder went straight up to the top of the tower. When I got to that part of the ladder it looked to me like it was angled backward and that spooked me, so I started back down. All my buddies made it to the top except me. As I was halfway down the police showed up. Once again, I met with the Dean. This time I'm considered an official "troublemaker."

I got the speech, and the Dean read the rules to me. I had no defense. Had I made it to the top I probably wouldn't have gotten caught. None of my friends were caught and I didn't rat them out. I was concerned that this time they were going to call my parents. But again, that didn't happen. I was confined to my dorm room and the Dorm Monitor checked to make sure I was there unless I was in class or eating. They let me finish the semester, but my college career at Concord was over. The next Fall, I entered Beckley College, where I got a two-year Associates

Degree in 1969.

I played a little when I was in college, mainly as a fill-in musician from time to time but the desire to play remained strong. After college I started working a demanding job at a funeral home and driving an ambulance, making it almost impossible to play.

CHAPTER 5: MUSIC OR EMBALMING

My relationship with Judi developed over the previous two years so we decided to get married. I was 19 and Judi was 17. It was well known that there was a town in Virginia named Pearisburg, where underage couples could get married. So, we made plans. Judi had been raised by her grand-parents and they knew about the marriage, but I didn't tell my parents. We set a date and headed to Pearisburg. Once we got there Judi messed up and told them she was 18 instead of 21. That killed the opportunity there, so we asked around and a couple told us we could do the same thing in Salem, Virginia, just down the road. So off we went, got our stories straight and we were married. That night I was on call at Keyser-Bryant Funeral Home in Beckley, West Virginia so we spent our first night together at the funeral home in the room next to the morgue. How romantic.

My time at Keyser-Bryant Funeral Home was so much fun. Doug Bryant, the owner hired Sam Ratliff a classmate of mine and Mike Goode who graduated from a rival high school in Pineville, West Virginia. We were untrained ambulance drivers, car washers and janitors. Sam was a guy who mostly did things "by the book" while Mike and I were a little reckless. Sam would distance himself from Mike and me when we were doing things we shouldn't have been doing. He would look the other way and rarely participated in our escapades. I remember one night Mike and I got an ambulance call and Mike tipped the ambulance up on two wheels going around a turn.

There was also a character named Noah Raines who worked at a rival funeral home across town. We had all become friends via seeing each other at hospital emergency rooms. On more than one occasion Noah would call us and say, "Hey boys you want to go to Burger Boy and get a burger." We couldn't leave the funeral home unless we got an ambulance call so Noah would make a fake call to the police that there was a wreck at Burger Boy and we'd all head that way. Of course, there was no wreck, but the burgers were great.

By 1969, I had put together a new band and we were starting to get a local following. By then I was working at Rose & Quesenberry Funeral Home in Beckley, West Virginia, and I had booked us to play at a local club called "The Oxford Inn." It was a standalone club, so I don't know where the name "Inn" came from, but it was a hot spot at the time for bands. I was on call that night for the funeral home, but I hired Eugene Thompson, a former employee to cover for me. He had done that for others and me from time to time. The owners, Amos and Frances Quesenberry, were out of town that week and I didn't get a chance to ask if they were alright with Eugene covering for me. But their sons, David and Michael, gave me their blessing so I thought it would be okay.

David was a fun guy and often when Amos and Frances were out of town, David was known to have parties in their residence over the funeral home. That night was no exception other than David included Eugene, the person who was covering for me, in the party. There were other employees at the party too, but they were off-duty. Ultimately, I was the one that was responsible for being there.

At some point in the party Eugene offered up the idea that they should all go to "The Oxford Inn" to watch our band. Michael offered to stay at the funeral home and take any calls that may come in for an ambulance or a death. Remember, this was back in the day of the "beeper," so if they needed you, they could beep you and you would call in and see what they needed. The club was only a few miles from the funeral home, so Eugene decided to take the ambulance in case he got a call. He parked it on the sidewalk right in the front door of the club. He had hit the curb so hard he flattened the tire although he didn't realize it until he left the club to go home.

So here was the scenario: I'm playing in the band at "The Oxford Inn"; Eugene, David and other employees were inside the club partying; and Michael was at the funeral home to answer the phone. For some reason, Amos and Frances decided to come home early. On their way to the funeral home Amos saw his ambulance sitting at the front door of "The Oxford Inn." Since I'm on call, Amos thought I'd been called there due to someone being hurt, but he noticed the ambulance had a flat tire. Amos and Frances continued to their residence at the funeral home, to find the place trashed from the party and Michael ratted us out. I didn't hear anything about it until the next morning when I went to work and found out Amos had fired all of us. It was another instance of playing music costing me a job.

By 1970, I had finished two years at Beckley College and had done a one-year apprenticeship at the funeral home and headed to Louisville, Kentucky, to attend Mortuary School at Kentucky School of Mortuary Science. Louisville was a wake-up call for someone like me who had grown up fairly isolated in West Virginia. I grew up a lot in that year and there were some lean times when Judi and I scraped the bottom of a peanut butter jar. Heck, one time one of my classmates from South Carolina went to a city park and killed a squirrel that we skinned, cleaned and shared among several of us.

I put music on hold while I was in school because of the intense curriculum to become a funeral director and embalmer. I graduated in 1971, and Judi and I welcomed our first son, Richard, into the world.

I had taken a job at Honaker-Harris Funeral Home in Logan, West Virginia, where I experienced a life-changing event. The day after my birthday, on February 26, 1972, a horrendous disaster struck a few miles up the road from Logan, on Buffalo Creek, near Man, West Virginia. A coal-mining dam had collapsed flooding several communities along its 15-mile path. The flood left more than 4,000 people homeless, 1,100 injured and it killed 125 men, women and children.

I was visiting my parents near Beckley when I got the call. The following morning I returned to Logan and then had to go to Man, about 10 miles away, where they had set up a temporary morgue at the Man Junior High School gym. In my years as an ambulance driver and working at funeral homes, I had seen a lot of terrible things, but I wasn't prepared for what I was about to see.

Because the water behind the dam was used to clean coal, it was black and had a silty consistency. As I approached the entrance to the morgue, I noticed refrigerated trucks in the parking lot where unidentified bodies could be preserved for several days. There were a few bodies in the parking lot being cleaned with hoses to remove as much of the black silt that covered their bodies before being placed in the gym to be identified. As I entered, the sight weakened me. Row after row of bodies on display for identification by relatives or friends. There were a lot of children and that sight alone was heart wrenching. Clothing had been ripped from many of them. You could see tree branches impaled in their bodies where they had been tumbled over and over. It left an indelible image in my brain that I can still see to this day and it made me realize this may not be my calling in life.

A few months after the flood, I was offered a position in Charleston, West Virginia, with Cunningham Funeral Home. Jim Cunningham, the owner, was a young, energetic man, a great person and a music lover. He and I hit it off, and when he found out I knew a lot about the music business he expressed an interest in buying an old theater and turning it into a music venue. We talked about it for a few months and then he made the move.

The theater was located on Charleston's west side and since it had been idle for some time it was in rough condition. I told Jim he would need to rearrange the backstage for dressing rooms, address some acoustical issues, and install sound and lighting. I don't think he realized the time and money it was going to take. But the next thing I know my duties at the funeral home were put on hold and my job title changed to consultant, janitor, carpenter and painter. I was loving the fact that I was involved in a music related venture and that I would be rubbing elbows with some big-time country stars. We spent two or three months of hard labor to get the place ready. There were still areas of wet paint when it opened on January 20, 1973. The venue was called the "Capitol City Jamboree" and it was off and running.

Jim didn't hold back on spending money for talent and major country stars from Nashville and the Wheeling Jamboree headlined the shows. People such as Joe Stampley, Barbara Fairchild, Tex Ritter and West Virginia's own Mel Street. There were local acts as well who would open the show and it had the feel of the Grand Ole Opry.

The opening acts were from the area but were really impressive. I remember The Heckel Family, George Daugherty, who played the musical saw, and a bluegrass trio called "The Hillbreed." They were all big hits with the audiences and it was a great time.

CHAPTER 6: MANAGER AND AGENT

One of the local acts performing at the Capitol City Jamboree was a bluegrass band called "The Hillbreed." The group was made up of James Harrison on banjo, Randy Tyler on acoustic guitar and Al Davidson on the bass. They were more than musicians and singers and they had developed an act that I thought could have national success. All three were witty and funny and their personalities were a perfect blend on stage, both musically and comedic. Al was kind of the spokesman for the band on stage and James was the brunt of his jokes. Randy just tried to stay out of the way. I started looking for ways to help them and I got them booked in Washington, D.C., at a party for the Georgetown Day School. This was a school where the rich and affluent people of Washington sent their kids, including Ted and Bobby Kennedy and many of their colleagues in the House and Senate. I was concerned we were going to be as "out of place" as you could imagine at an event like that.

Our first problem was how to get there. Somebody showed up with an old van that was stripped out on the inside. We ended up putting a normal size bed in the back so two people could ride on the bed and the other two could sit up front. As we started the trip, there was always banter between us. On this trip Randy and I were giving James a hard time about being overweight. We had been making "fat jokes" but Al was unusually quiet. Al was in the back on the bed and had consumed some kind of substance that had him in a calm, laid back state. He would usually jump right in when we were messing with James. This time, he hadn't said a word. James was driving and had been defending himself when he said, "I hope you guys have enjoyed all this, but at least I have one real friend in this van and that's Al. He hasn't said a word about my weight. Ain't that right Al?" to which Al replied, "That's right lard ass."

Al was known to partake of "wacky tobacky" and had found some really good "weed" that mellowed him out on this trip. However, it didn't dull his senses enough to jump in and give James a dig. He did forget the cable to plug in his bass on this trip and, on another trip, he actually forgot to bring his bass.

One of the scariest times on the road happened on that same trip home from Washington, D.C. There was a big semi right on our rear. James was driving and he when he would slow down hoping the truck would pass us, the truck would slow down as well. We made a quick exit and thought we had lost him. When we got back on, he was waiting at the bottom of the entrance ramp and fell right in behind us again. I asked James if he had done anything that would have upset the driver. James said he hadn't. About that time, Al spoke up and said he had been giving the driver the one finger salute because he was riding our bumper and his headlights were too bright. The game of cat and mouse went on for miles and miles until there was a split and the driver went one direction, and we went the other. It was a scary time, but Al was again quiet until just the right time to confess. Whatever he had procured to smoke was very effective.

I was having moderate success at booking "The Hillbreed" and I started taking on other acts. Eventually I opened an agency called "Talent Enterprises" and at one time I had about 17 acts on my roster. I decided to move the agency back home to Beckley to cut costs. I started working with a popular rock 'n' roll band called "Quint," based in Huntington, West Virginia. The band was very popular in the early '70s in the area. They sounded great and their professionalism on stage was incredible, but there was one problem. They always paid me my commission late.

I had them booked at a hot nightclub in Huntington, so I decided I would outsmart them and make the two-hour drive to Huntington and collect my commission on the spot when they got paid at the end of the night.

When I arrived, they all looked surprised to see me, but they welcomed me, and we were having a great time. This was a monumental day in my life, because this day would be the biggest reason I never did drugs. Every time the band took a break, we would step out to the van where they would smoke pot and we would talk about plans for the band. After the third set, we went to the van and they kept pushing me to take a toke off a joint. I gave it a try and didn't really feel any different, so I did another and another. I don't remember getting high. I don't remember a gradual segue to feeling grand. The next thing I remember was waking up in my bed at home in Beckley and it was Monday morning. I left Huntington sometime late Saturday night, but I didn't remember driving home.

I vaguely remember passing a series of trucks and it was like they would pass me, rewind and pass me again. The scariest part was that I had to stop and pay two tolls on the way home. I didn't remember that either. It scared me to death. From that day on, I never took a pill or did drugs ever again. To top it all off, the band didn't pay me that night and I had to wait on my commission again. So, all in all, that night was a complete waste of time other than the lesson I learned.

CHAPTER 7: DYING TO PLAY BASS

In 1973, I got a call from a guy who managed a bar band who told me his bass player was going to take a two-week vacation and asked if I could fill in on bass. I had never played bass, didn't own a bass and I told him that. He said he couldn't find a bass player and asked if I would give it a shot. Since I didn't own a bass guitar or amplifier, I called my friends at Jan Campbell Music and they let me borrow a bass and an amp for two weeks. Try doing that with a music store these days.

I messed around with it a few days, and having played guitar for eight years, playing the bass felt very natural to me. The places we were playing were what some musicians call "gun and knife" clubs. In other words, you needed to be carrying one or the other if you played there. The guy who managed the band always had a gun in his pocket, so I considered that somewhat good. But since I didn't know how well he could shoot or his temperament, it worried me a lot too. Keep in mind the guy managing the band was not in the band. He was the band manager, because he owned the PA system and a van.

There were lots of fights and altercations and I saw guns drawn and a stabbing or two. These clubs were really rough and the first thing I learned as I went into these establishments was to find the exit and plan a way to escape in case there was trouble. I still do that today.

One night we were playing a bar in Eccles, West Virginia. It was probably the worst place I ever played. Trust me, that's saying a lot. It was dark, dirty and right in the middle of the dance floor was a standalone potbelly coal stove. In the winter it would be so hot it would glow red. I saw a few "pleather" coats and jackets get scorched and melted where someone would stagger into the stove or get pushed into it. It was a scary setup.

At the end of the night the guy managing the band and the

lead singer got into an argument over money. It was a typical scenario where the manager would get the money and distribute it to the band members. On this night the lead singer discovered the manager got paid a lot more than he told us. In other words, the manager didn't do an even cut on the money. It was fine with me since he gave me what he promised me, but the singer didn't see it that way. They started yelling at each other and as the argument got worse and worse, the manager pulled out his gun and stuck it right up to the nose of the singer. Fortunately, the singer backed down and the altercation ended. But not before someone called the police. As I started tearing down my equipment about six West Virginia State Troopers came through the door with guns drawn and took the band manager into custody. Once they had him in handcuffs the police demanded everybody leave. I tried to explain I needed to get my equipment, but they were having none of it and threw everybody out of the building. I was sitting in my car wondering how in the world I was going to get my gear and also thinking Judi is going to kill me because I wasn't going to get home when she expected. Finally, the troopers started coming out of the building and I explained that I needed to get my equipment. One of them escorted me in and out as I got my stuff.

When I got home that night, I couldn't sleep. That event really frightened me, and I figured if this manager would kill the lead singer, then a bass player wouldn't be safe at all. I made up my mind I was not going to play at that level ever again. I called the manager and quit the band the next day.

A few days later I got a call from a drummer who had heard me play and asked if I would be interested in playing in a Gospel band. The timing for that call was perfect and I jumped at the opportunity. We were backing four sisters known as the "Gospel Belles" who had great sibling harmony. I bought a van and we played locally and traveled on weekends when necessary. It was a good way to get my mind off that last bar gig and put me in a safe environment. Mark Carman, who was 15 at the time, was the piano player in the band. Later on, Mark found his way to

Nashville where we reconnected. Since then, he has been nominated for a Grammy and was head of the Nashville office for Cashbox Magazine.

CHAPTER 8: THE DORIS KING BAND

In 1974, I got a call from Jerry King, a drummer and husband of Doris King, a well-known and talented local singer. He asked if I would be interested in joining the band. Doris was known for playing classy gigs and this seemed like a way to up my game as a local musician. Doris and Jerry lived in a beautiful home in Mabscott, West Virginia, and we rehearsed just down the street at Jerry's mother's house. She had a big basement, and she let us leave our equipment set up there and rehearse once or twice a week.

I started helping Jerry with booking the band and I got us a lucrative New Year's Eve gig at a posh country club in Lexington, Kentucky. I had never gotten this much money for a gig and never played at such an exclusive venue. It catered to a lot of millionaires, including some well-known thoroughbred horse owners. I was extremely excited and as the gig got closer I kept telling the band what a big deal this was going to be for the band.

We were all a little nervous, but I was confident that Doris would be perfect for this crowd and would win them over immediately. We had worked several country clubs in Virginia and West Virginia, and she was always a hit.

We had a young guitar player named Jack Williams. Jack was a nervous type guy back then, but a great guitar player. The day we were leaving to go to Lexington, Jerry and I went over to his mother's house to get his drums and my bass gear. Jack was supposed to meet us there, but when we arrived, Jack's equipment was already gone. That puzzled Jerry so he went upstairs and asked his mother if Jack had come early and gotten his gear. She replied, "no." A call to Jack got no answer.

At that point we're getting a little concerned. We started questioning how this could have happened. Where was his equipment? Did someone steal it? Why would they only take his stuff? There was a doggy door in the garage, but surely no one could fit through that. Jerry went upstairs and again tried to call Jack and some of his friends to see if anyone knew what was going on. Finally, somebody told Jerry that Jack wasn't going to do the gig. He had, in fact, gone through the doggy door to get his equipment and did it all without Jerry's mother hearing him.

At that moment Jerry and I panicked. It was the biggest show we've ever done, and we have a few hours to find a guitar player and get on the road. One of Doris's former guitar players, Rodger Cozart, lived a few streets over so Jerry called him and, even though it was last minute, he agreed to bail us out. He even had one of his old ruffled band shirts to wear. God was smiling down on us, since Rodger knew most of the songs and had worked with Doris before. He also knew how to handle himself in a professional manner. The show went beautifully; we got tipped an extra $1,000 by one of the club members and we played there several times. I didn't speak to Jack for a long time after that.

I also booked us at another prestigious spot as the house band at Pipestem State Park and Resort. It was a beautiful spot nestled in the mountains about an hour south of Beckley. Again, it was a perfect fit for Doris, and we did such a wide variety of material that it was hard to stump the band. We had two great keyboard players, Bobby Holley and Ronnie Wells, who worked with us at different times. I really enjoyed working for Doris and Jerry and we had a lot of fun.

The band worked at every opportunity. Even though I this was Jerry's band, I found myself getting involved in the business side of things again and I was able to get us more gigs so we were able to play more often.

CHAPTER 9: MUSIC OR
THE COAL MINES

As my life continued to evolve in West Virginia, the logical spot for me to make good money and provide for my family was working at a coal mine. Judi was pregnant with our second son, Robert, and my responsibility to my family became a priority.

The State of West Virginia mandated that each coalmine have an Emergency Medical Technician (EMT) on site. Since I was driving an ambulance I had an EMT license and a lot of emergency training. My Dad got me on board with Ranger Fuel who had coalmines in Bolt, West Virginia.

Since the job as EMT involved mainly sitting around waiting on someone to get hurt, the company trained me to do other things. The first thing was to be an environmentalist that had me doing dust and noise level testing inside the mine and on the surface to stay in compliance with state and federal regulations. I would also conduct safety meetings and first-aid classes for the miners and I trained as a part of the Mine Rescue & First Aid Team. Later I became a mine inspector for the company, citing violations inside the mines and on the surface. The idea was that I would find violations in advance of federal or state mine inspectors who showed up randomly. The money, the benefits, and the retirement and stock programs were great.

Once I took the job at the mines, I decided to stop playing music for a while until I could see if the new job would require a lot of my time. In the beginning that was true. As I learned the ropes and got my certifications at the mine, I realized that I would be free most every weekend and I decided to put together a new band.

I called Jack Williams, the guitar player, and Ronnie Wells, the keyboard player, I had worked with in Doris King's band and they agreed to come on board. Someone gave me the name and number for Keith Kittle, a drummer who had played with some of the area's top bands. We were set. We got together a few times and there

RANGER FUEL MINE RESCUE TEAM

was a good vibe, and the band came together pretty quickly. I was impressed with the talent in the band and it gave me reason to call the band, "Visions", in keeping with my dream that this could become that band in my dreams. The name was a reminder that gave me hope that one day maybe this band and I could do this full time.

It wasn't long until I had us working weekends and making good money. One of the big reasons for our success was we could do a wide variety of material, so we were able to play just about any gig that came along. Our song list covered songs from the '40s to the current hits, so we could play a swanky job at the Black Knight Country Club, a high school or college dance, a country bar, or rock 'n' roll and disco at a night club. We dressed alike, depending on the job, including tuxedos and ruffled shirts for the high dollar gigs we played.

Ronnie was a foreman for a construction company and as his job became more demanding, he had to leave the band. Jack Williams' cousin, Jimmy Furrow played keyboards and Jack persuaded Jimmy to join us. Jimmy was a talented guy and knew a lot of songs, so he fit right in.

One night we played a private fund-raising party in Charleston for a political party and got paid quite a bit of money. We decided to go to an expensive restaurant and have steaks in Charleston - a big deal for Beckley boys. Again, here we are a little out of place and ignorant to a lot of the ways of the world and here's the proof. As we ordered, one of the guys ordered a Halibut steak and when it came out, he was complaining to the waitress that it wasn't done and was white inside. She informed him it was fish, not beef.

As we progressed, I had seen a band using lights and pyrotechnics (fire) and I thought it might be cool if we did the same. My Dad helped me put together a lighting system made of old coffee cans. I took two of the big coffee cans, taped them together with duct tape and spray painted them flat black. We wired the cans to hold colored floodlights and made some brackets and stands. My Dad built a lighting board so Greg Hungate our young sound guy could run the sound and lights from the soundboard.

In addition to the lights, I found there was a substance called flash powder that magicians often use in their acts that would give off a big flash when ignited. It was expensive so we decided to mix it with a little gunpowder - actually a lot of gunpowder. I had rigged up a fuse that would burn through once power was applied to it and set off the mixture. I used porcelain light sockets, and I put a fuse in the bottom and poured the gunpowder and flash powder into the light socket on top of the fuse. I had a wire rigged to the soundboard and a push button detonator on the soundboard so Greg could hit the button at the appropriate time and fire and smoke would shoot up. It looked and sounded amazing.

We had a gig at Glen Rogers High School, about 20 miles from Beckley. We thought the young crowd would love the pyrotechnics, so we decided to wire it up for that show. We placed a pot on each side of the stage. We decided to do a test before anyone got to the school and Keith Kittle our drummer was helping me make sure they were working properly. The first time I hit the button, the flash went off on the left side of the stage but the right one failed. Keith went over to check the fuse and just as he was leaning forward it went off and barely missed him. That concerned me because it was certainly an unsafe situation, especially if it happened again. After the first test, Keith determined we needed more gunpowder, so we reloaded and did a second test that went well, other than the mushroom cloud going to the ceiling and the smell of gunpowder. It was getting close to showtime, so we loaded the pots up for a big shot at the end of our show.

When we took our first break, there were kids hanging around the stage and all around the gym. At some point during that break a kid accidentally leaned on the light board and pushed the button that set off the pyrotechnics. There were several kids near the pots and the noise, flash and smoke scared everybody in the building. Some of the kids closest to the pots could have been severely injured but thank God they weren't. Needless to say, we discontinued using pyrotechnics in the show. The lights worked great.

We had some interesting gigs in West Virginia and not every place we played was considered safe. Occasionally we played a club in Webster Springs, West Virginia, called The U Turn. The club was located just before you got to the main town and was in the sharpest curve I ever saw in West Virginia. The club was in an area known for rough and tough coal miners, lumberjacks and bikers. There were fistfights and yelling, but I don't ever remember there being a major incident inside the club. It was a definitely a volatile mix of people and a place where you had to keep an eye on what was going on.

One weekend we were booked there on a Friday and Saturday night. We got a room at a local motel for Friday night since it was a two-hour drive from home, and we decided to stay Friday night in Webster Springs. At the end of the gig on Friday night, somebody in the band invited some bikers and their girlfriends to our motel room. It was not a good idea. We didn't have a lot of money so all five of us were staying in one room and having a party with 10 more people put us in close proximity with our party guests. In the room next door to us were a couple of salesmen from Pennsylvania that we met when we checked in and invited them to come and see us at the club. After the show, we all got back to the motel at the same time and the sales guys came in our room for the after party along with four bikers and their girlfriends. At one point there were 15 people in our room.

The bikers had beer, whiskey and other stuff, so we had a full-blown party. I believe the motel was empty or we would have been kicked out. But we never got a call from the manager and the police didn't show up so everything was cool, and no one was out of line.

In the wee hours of the morning, I remember one of the bikers say to the others, "Let's ride," which meant as far as they were concerned the party was over. Since I didn't drink or do drugs, I was happy and relieved they would be leaving.

Then one of the biker girls said, "I'm not ready to leave. I'm gonna stay here and party." The other girls chimed in that they were going to stay too. There was some grumbling, and finally one of the bikers got mad and said, "By God if they want to stay, let's just leave them here." That's not what I wanted to hear, but nobody said anything, so the bikers left. The two salesmen left at the same time and went to their room next door.

As the party wore down, people were falling asleep or passing out, so I'm thinking I'm finally going to get some rest. I had worked all day on Friday, and I was wiped out physically.

About thirty minutes later we heard the rumble of motorcycles. The bikers had returned to the hotel to get their women. I don't know how many there were, but it was definitely more than four. The headlights from the bikes glared into the window shades and with motors revving one of the bikers rolled up to the door where the salesmen were staying and started yelling, "Tell the girls to get out here." The salesmen were scared and wouldn't open the door. A biker yelled, "We've come to get our women and if you don't open that door, I'm going to ride through it."

I told everybody to be quiet and get in the floor. We were scared to death. This is not the way I want to die. Luckily, one of the salesmen opened the door and said, "The girls have already left." The biker went in their room, took a look around and then they all rumbled out of the parking lot. That night a lesson was learned about not inviting people to our room after the show, especially drunken and drugged up bikers.

One of our favorite gigs was the Strawberry Festival in Buckhannon, West Virginia. It was big event, and I was able to develop a relationship with Brad Kellison who booked entertainment for the festival. He used us every year at a couple of venues over the weekend and it was always a fun time for us. Over the years I got to play behind Richard Kline who played Larry Dallas on the TV series "Three's Company," members of the cast from "The Dukes Of Hazzard"— Catherine Bach (Daisy Duke) and John Schneider (Bo Duke)—and Anson Williams (Potsie Weber) from "Happy Days."

One night after our last show at the festival, Jack, the guitar player and I started home to Beckley. Back then it was a winding 130-mile drive through the mountains to Beckley. About halfway there, my headlights went out. It was pitch black and desolate and instead of us sitting there until morning, I decided to drive home using only the amber park lights to see. It was a long, slow process but we made it. Another experience Jack or I will never forget.

Then came an instance where my playing nearly cost me my job at the coalmine. It was 1978 and I had booked the band on a Friday and Saturday night at the Colonade nightclub in South Charleston, West Virginia. Normally my job at the mines was 9 to 5, Monday through Friday. If I had weekend gigs, I would leave work Friday evening clean up and go play. Normally the gigs were close to Beckley, but the Charleston gig was an hour down the road and after working all day Friday and then playing 9 pm to 1 am, I decided I would spend the night in Charleston and rest up before the gig on Saturday night.

Occasionally, if the coalmine had mechanical issues or their production numbers were down, they would schedule work on Saturdays to make up for lost down time. It didn't happen too often and, in the past, if I was playing on a Friday night near Beckley I could still work on Saturday. This weekend we were playing more than an hour from home so I decided to take the chance of not going to work on Saturday, hoping nothing would happen where I would be missed. It was not a good decision.

That Saturday, one of the miners got his sleeve caught in a piece of machinery and it literally pulled his arm off. It was an extremely bad accident and they immediately started calling for me. I was not there. The company had another mine 10 miles up the road and my counterpart at that mine, Larry Bane was on duty. He went to the mine and covered for me. When I got home Sunday morning, I had a voice message from Larry telling me what happened. I called him and we discussed it further, but I really had no legitimate excuse for not being there. I didn't tell anybody beforehand that I was going to play music and I wouldn't be at work. I felt horrible for the injured miner and his family, but I was also worried this might cost me my job. If I had told my boss he probably would have given me the day off, but I didn't do that and I was totally in the wrong. Thank God the miner didn't die, but he could have.

I dreaded the ride to work on Monday morning, and as soon as I pulled into the parking lot, the mine superintendent Len Proffitt called me to his office. I didn't lie to him and gave him the whole story, apologizing as I went. Len wasn't my boss. My boss, Stewart Deck, had an office in Beckley about an hour away, but he did come to the scene of the accident on that Saturday and was asking if anyone knew where I was. Len told Stewart he had given me permission to be off that Saturday. That saved my job. I was so relieved and grateful to Len for what he did for me, but I still carry the guilt of not being there for that miner who needed me. That incident pretty much sealed the deal for me that I needed to get away from the mines. I kept asking myself, "What if that miner had been in a scenario where me not being there could have cost him his life?" I was torn between my music and this job, so I made a decision.

CHAPTER 10: VISIONS - THE BAND

I knew that working a day job provided money and security, but I was constantly thinking about music and where I'd be playing next. I wasn't happy at work and my obsession with music had caused me to put someone's life in jeopardy. I decided life was too short to spend it feeling this way, so I put together a plan to quit my job and go on the road playing music full time. I worked hard for two years to get the band ready and in a position to be considered by agents and talent buyers as a professional road band. My plan began to take shape.

I kept my plan to myself in case things didn't work out. I didn't want people saying, "I told you so," and I didn't want the band members to be disappointed if I failed. I didn't even tell my wife, although she knew how I hated to get up at 6 am and drive to the coalmines. And she knew how much I loved my music. Thank God she supported me for the most part.

Once I determined the band was ready, we had a meeting and I laid out my plan. After answering a lot of their questions (and their family's questions), they all agreed to give it a try. It wasn't a popular decision with some family members who didn't consider music a career, but we were determined to show them different.

The next step in my plan was lining up a booking agent. I quickly discovered agents weren't interested in booking us, since we were a local weekend band who didn't have experience on the road. Fortunately, I had the phone number of Bill Heaberlin, an agent that had booked a show or two for one of my previous bands. Bill had a company called Media Promotions based in Huntington, West Virginia, about 120 miles away. When I called him, he remembered me and, even though he was two hours away, I convinced him to come and see the band. We were playing at the Ramada Inn in Beckley in their show club called

"The Velvet Mine." It was a hot spot in Beckley and hosted show bands from all across the country. I would go see these bands and steal their show ideas and comedy. Bill was impressed with the band but recommended we add a front man to give us more of a "showy" commercial look and sound.

So, we put the word out through a musician's referral service and found a guy named Bobby Johnson, a tall African American who was quite an entertainer and singer. He was one of those people who could capture an audience and have them eating out of the palm of his hand. We did a lot of Motown and R & B songs before Bobby came along, but boy what a difference he made to the versatility and showmanship of the band. It really increased my confidence that this was going to work.

As a touring band during c that time, we would be traveling every two to three weeks, playing what was called the "Ramada Inn Circuit" in lounges and show rooms in hotels. It was popular among road bands because you could see the country, settle in a town for a couple of weeks, and make a decent living without having the expenses, physical wear and tear on your body, and traveling every day. That type of touring no longer exists because of stricter drunk driving laws, coupled with more entertainment options.

Everybody in the band had a car, but if we were going on the road, we needed vans. I was married with two children, so I opted for a small motor home - A Dodge Trans Van. The drummer was also married so he traded his car for a van so he could take his wife. The guitar player and the keyboard player were cousins so they shared a van and occasionally the guitar player's girlfriend would travel with him. Bobby, the lead singer was already set up for the road and had a box truck modified for music and travel.

My biggest fear in going on the road was telling my parents. Even though I was 30 years old, I knew this was not going to be easy. Like most parents, they were not optimistic about my future as a musician. I think I had exceeded their expectations by what I had accomplished at a local level, but they were very skeptical that my "plan" and the band would succeed on the road. I had a great day job, was making good money with bene-fits and retirement and, in their mind, I was going to throw that all away. Really? Yes, really. My uncles Hester and Remus were also musicians and they did

KEITH KITTLE   JACK WILLIAMS   JIMMY FURROW   DICK MCVEY

their best to support my dreams, but most everybody else thought I was crazy.

Unfortunately, that "can't do" culture exists across this nation and it discourages many talented people from follow-ing their dreams. When I was young, I was taught you get an education, get a job, and work until you die. Anytime I men-tioned playing on the road or possibly moving to Nashville, people laughed and said I wouldn't have a chance. My Dad later confided that he was afraid I would get involved in drugs and alcohol—I never did either. It was because of the way he raised me, and when I told him I got my kicks from playing music that seemed to calm his fears and we were off to our first gig about a month later.

Before we left town, our hometown decided to throw a big going away party and we performed a farewell show at the "Vel-vet Mine." It was a packed house and most of our friends and fans were there. They seemed proud that hometown boys were hitting the road as professional musicians. In fact, there were several girls there that night to see our guitar player off. The problem was they didn't realize each other existed. He came to me before the show and confessed that he was in a pickle. So, we devised a plan that every time we took a break he would head to the bathroom or a room we had rented at the Ramada Inn, and the other band members would tell the girls he was really sick. It worked for that night at least.

As we prepared to leave town, we received a surprise. Each of us was presented with an official certificate from the State of

West Virginia proclaiming us as "Ambassadors of Music" for the state. That was quite an honor for each of us to be representing West Virginia on our musical journey.

CHAPTER 11: VISIONS
- ON THE ROAD

One of the proudest and most exciting days of my life was hitting the road with the band. Our first gig was in Florence, South Carolina, at a motel that had a nice lounge.

Most of the road gigs gave us five rooms at the hotel and some of them offered food or a discount in the hotel restaurant. Our days were free, but we normally rehearsed two or three times a week and played six nights each week. We spent a lot of time exploring the towns where we played and at the swimming pool - a perk the kids loved. Sunday was usually our night off and our typical hours were 8 pm to midnight on weeknights and 9 pm to 1 or 2 am on Fridays and Saturdays. My wife home schooled our oldest son Richard via an accredited home school program. Our pay then was $1,800 to $2,300 per week and we did an even split on the money, which meant we made $350 to $450 each per week. Our average pay of $400 per week back then is equivalent to $1,400 in today's money. That number is scary considering musicians aren't making much more than they did back in 1979 and yet the cost of living had quadrupled. It felt like we were actually living the dream.

My primary job on the road was keeping everybody happy. By that I mean keeping band members motivated and getting along; keeping the club managers happy; keeping the customers happy; and most of all, doing our part to "make the cash registers ring" at the clubs. I found out a long time ago that if the clubs were making money, we were making money and that insured return visits to that club.

I would research the Billboard charts to see what songs were popular that we could perform live. We played songs people wanted to hear whether we liked them or not. I guess if there are two things musicians don't like about their jobs, it's they don't like playing songs they don't like and they don't like playing songs they've played hundreds of times and don't enjoy playing anymore. Luckily, I had musicians who understood that if they wanted to work, it was important to give the people what they wanted.

Our first big problem on the road developed over money. When we formed the band, the idea was that every member would take an even split. If we made $2,000, we'd each made $400. The front man thought he deserved more. I tried to reason with him by telling him the band had the same expenses as he did and that the band owned and was providing all the equipment he needed to do the show. He disagreed and when it turned into an argument, I fired him. I sensed this was coming and had already alerted the agent that it might happen. The agent agreed to continue booking us as a four-piece band, but it was much harder to do without a bonafide front man. Without Bobby we really didn't have a show and since hotels were looking for show bands, we had to work lounges at a lower level for a few weeks. Luckily Jack, Keith and I could all sing and we knew enough songs on our own to pull it off, but we really needed a front man.

We played our first show as a four-piece band at the Ramada Inn in Bath, New York, and were scheduled to play Snowshoe Ski Resort near Marlington, West Virginia, right after that. The show in Marlington would have given us the opportunity to commute to and from the gig from our homes. The plan was that we would reconnect with our families while doing the gigs in Marlington. We were looking forward to seeing family and friends and sleeping in our own beds for a change. The wives and girlfriend decided they wouldn't go to New York since we would only be gone for two weeks. They were tired of the travel and living out of a suitcase, so they decided to go home while we did the New York gig.

A few days before we were set to travel to West Virginia the roof on the ski resort collapsed and they cancelled us. Now we had nowhere to play. The agent was scrambling, the band was panicking, and I'm begging him to find us a gig. And he did—in Tampa, Florida. We had one day to get there, and it was 1,200 miles and 20 hours away. We had been playing in Ohio and New York where it was cold so the thought of going to Florida was a welcome idea. The wives and girlfriend were not happy, but they supported us, and our decision not to come home. We finished in New York and headed to Florida. We got there dog-tired but managed to get through the first night and got some rest. I doubt we were very good that night, but we didn't get fired, so I assume we were adequate. None of us could remember.

Tampa was a blessing and a curse. It was three weeks in the sunshine of Florida, but the female club manager was not very nice to us. I assumed she treated all bands like that since she had fired the band before us and that's why the gig became available to us on short notice. I made a special effort to be nice to her. We had a meeting the day after we got there to go over her "rules" and schedule time for us to rehearse. Right off the bat she told us she didn't allow bands to rehearse because it would disturb the guests. I had never heard that one before and, as nice as I could be, explained that if every venue was like that the bands would never learn any new songs. She reiterated, "No rehearsal." Her other rules were standard things so there wasn't any other dispute about that.

Just down the street from the hotel was an adult bookstore and since we had never been to one, our curiosity got the best of us, so Keith and I went to see what this was all about. When we got inside there were all kinds of magazines and toys, and in the back  was a series of booths where you could go inside and watch movies. The booths were small and there was only supposed to be one person at a time in each booth, but Keith and I decided we could cram in a booth together to save money. It cost a quarter for three minutes of viewing time. We didn't really look at the titles we just went down the row booth to booth. Every time we left a booth there was usually somebody waiting or standing in the hallway. We had taken in a few, but then we ended up in one showing gay guys. Keith said, "Let's get outta here." We argued for a minute or two as to whether we should walk out together which would make us seem gay. We finally decided we'd go out together. As we left that booth, I got a lot of strange looks. It was quite embarrassing and our last movie of the day, and our last trip to an adult bookstore.

We played the first week of three and got a great response. Toward the end of our second week, Jack's brother Sammy drove over to hang out and see the band. Sammy pulled up a stool at the bar and there was a loud New Yorker sitting beside him. Their conversation started out friendly enough but when the guy said something to Sammy about the band being "a bunch of hillbillies from West Virginia," Sammy hit him. There were two casualties of the fight. Our drummer Keith (who tried to break it up got his nose busted), and the band. We got fired.

This was the first place that I had ever been fired, and it was especially hurtful since it was for something we didn't do. It was also the first and only place that wouldn't let us rehearse. For those two reasons, I was very upset. I went to the supermarket and bought the biggest fresh fish I could find—it was big. When we went back to the club to get our equipment, I slid that big old fish in the ceiling on top of the ceiling tiles. It's one of the few revenge jokes I ever played where I wasn't able to see the results. Still, I've imagined many times what happened in the days that followed our departure and it still brings a smile to my face.

The good thing about Tampa was a booking agent from Orlando had stopped in for a drink and happened to see us and left us his card. I gave him a call and he made us an offer to put us with three singers and dancers and return to playing as a show band. He asked if we would be willing to take three weeks to re-hearse and get the show tight. We agreed to do that since getting fired from the Tampa job didn't set well with our agent and he didn't have another gig for us. So, it was either go home or try something new.

CHAPTER 12: THE SOLID GOLD BAND

After our bad experience in Tampa, we committed to working with Fred Weiss Productions (now Ted Skorman Productions) on a new show, and to back up a trio of singers/dancers. We traveled to Orlando where Mr. Weiss had rented rehearsal space for three weeks. He did not provide rooms or food for us, so we struggled to get by. Our wives were no longer traveling with us, and quite frankly they were not happy we were in Florida. They were dealing with cold weather in West Virginia and we were in sunny Florida, although we rarely saw the sun because we were inside rehearsing every day. They were also skeptical of our new plan and our calls home begging them to send us money from our savings was not met with great enthusiasm. In the end, the wives and families came through for us, but there were times we were living on a diet of peanut butter sandwiches and scraping the bottom of the jar.

All four of us were in a small motel room in Orlando and while we were there the first space shuttle was scheduled to lift off. It was Sunday morning, April 12, 1981, and we were all glued to the TV watching the launch when we heard a noise in the parking lot. When we looked outside, people were shouting and looking toward the sky. I ran onto the balcony in my underwear to see what the fuss was all about. You could actually see the shuttle going up with the naked eye. I was shocked it was visible, but happy that I could witness such a historical event, live as it happened.

Our schedule with Fred Weiss and Ted Skorman was grueling. We rehearsed 12 hours a day, 7 days a week. Fred or Ted would be with us the entire time so there was no slacking. I think they gave us one day off during those three weeks.

The idea for this band was to emulate a television show called "Solid Gold" which featured bands performing with "the Solid Gold" singers and dancers on stage with them. The three people who would be joining us were a male singer/dancer who was married to a female singer/dancer and there was another female singer/dancer.

For the first seven days of rehearsal, it was just the band. Fred told us not to worry about messing up the music while we played the songs but to change our focus to smiling and moving on every song. He wanted a lot more stage energy from us as the band. I can't tell you how many times we heard him yell, "Smile and move...smile and move" over and over again.

After the first week the singers and dancers joined us, and we started learning their material. We never used charts; we learned the songs just like the records. The one thing that discouraged us was their vocals. They were just average. Fortunately, they had great colorful costumes and their dancing was spot on. And so, we rehearsed over and over and over, from 10 am to 10 pm every day and the show began to tighten up and look professional.

Our first gig was in Jacksonville, Florida at a huge nightclub. Once we hit the stage, we felt we owned that crowd. I found out that adrenalin and confidence are an extremely strong combination in performing a successful show, especially at this level, which was bigger and better than anything we had done before. We traveled the country, and the show was extremely successful and impressive. Of course, using the name of the TV show garnered us a lot of attention and people actually thought the singers/dancers were part of the show. Fred even had their costumes designed to match what millions saw on TV.

It seemed to me the show should be making a lot of money based on where we were playing and the size of the crowds but getting the agent to give us more money was a never-ending battle. Then, I accidentally found out what the dancers and singers were getting paid. I saw a check on the dresser of one of the female singers. Since I had asked the agent about more money and was refused, I went to the band members for a meeting. We decided this band wasn't going anywhere career-wise because there wasn't a strong singer in the group. We agreed once again to return to our four-piece roots and go back to our original agent.

CHAPTER 13: NASHVILLE
IS CALLING

We reunited with Bill Heaberlin, our original agent, and he started booking shows for us again. One of those gigs was a five-week stint in the lounge at the Holiday Inn on Briley Parkway in Nashville. We had always wanted to play Nashville and now we had the opportunity. There was a catch—a big catch. Because it was summer, and the tourists were flooding Nashville they didn't have any rooms for us. It turned out to be one of the hottest summers on record. We were sleeping in our vans at a campground where temperatures were over 100 degrees during the day and rarely dropped below 80 degrees at night. It. Was. Hot. Even the swimming pool at the campground felt like bathwater. Our wives were there, my kids were there, and it was miserable. But hey, we're playing in Nashville, Tennessee.

Back in the day when show bands were coming to the Ramada Inn in Beckley, I would go check out the bands to steal their ideas for our shows. I watched and learned what worked and what didn't, and it was extremely helpful when we put our show band together. During that time, I met a bass player named John Frost who was working in one of the top show bands that came through Beckley. John's band was based in Nashville and he told me if I ever came to Nashville to give him a call. When I called his mother answered and told me he was singing with a group called "The Four Guys" on the Grand Ole Opry and she would have him call me. I explained he wouldn't be able to call me since I was staying at the campground (no cell phones back then), but I told her I would try him again later. When I finally spoke to him, he asked if I wanted to go backstage at the Opry during one of their afternoon matinees. It was a dream come true for me and I found myself hanging out with some of country music's most famous artists. I was star struck, in awe of my surroundings and the people backstage. I was hooked.

For the previous year it had crossed my mind as we traveled across the country that I was getting older, but the crowds were staying the same age. I was 32 years old and our crowds were mainly in their early 20s. We were playing Top 40 and Disco music and I was starting to question just how long I was going to be able to get onstage without looking out of place. The one thing I saw with country music was longevity and being able to continue to play as I got older. Now, here I was in Nashville and backstage at the Grand Ole Opry, and I saw a lot of older musicians on stage. I decided to check out the possibilities.

After that matinee I discussed my ambitions with John who told me if I was serious that he would check around if see if he could help me. I found out quickly that having a friend in Nashville who was connected in the music business gave me a huge advantage. I owe my career in Nashville to John. He was a true friend who helped me in many ways to realize my dream.

When I got back to the campground, I called the band together for a meeting where I told them about my feelings. I told them I felt I needed to move to Nashville because I felt like I was getting too old to be playing club gigs on the road. They thought I was kidding, but eventually realized I was serious about making the move.

After the Nashville shows I gave the agent our two-week notice. We had two weeks at a club in Stillwater, Oklahoma, and I decided that after those gigs, I would leave the band and move to Nashville. I invited them all to make the move with me since they were all good enough to work at a high level in Nashville. Jimmy, the keyboard player decided he would make the move with my family and me and later on Keith, the drummer, would join us. Jimmy decided he didn't want to tour any longer, so his focus became songwriting and he ended up with an office job at BMI Nashville. Keith wanted to play so he and I worked together in Nashville club bands and in the studio.

CHAPTER 14: I'M ON THE GRAND OLE OPRY

After the Oklahoma shows I decided to go to West Virginia to spend some time with Mom, Dad and my Sister. While I was there, I got a call from my friend John Frost in Nashville. He had found out that Grand Ole Opry star Stonewall Jackson was looking for a bass player and he put my name in the hat. They wanted me to come to Nashville immediately for an audition. I packed as quickly as I could and headed to Music City. It was a nerve-wracking time, but I nailed the audition and got the job. I was scared to death, because this took me to a level that I had only imagined in my dreams.

Our first show was on Broadway in Nashville playing at Tootsie's Orchid Lounge, a world-famous Nashville club. It was crowded, loud and smoky, and the stage was small. It was hard to believe this was the big time based on the situation. We played that night and Stonewall announced we would be playing the Grand Ole Opry the following weekend. This took my anxiety and excitement to a new level. I was going to be playing the Grand Ole Opry.

We would be doing a song Stonewall had just recorded titled "Old Chunk Of Coal." The song would later become a hit for John Anderson, but it was doing well for Stonewall at the time. I probably practiced that song 500 times over the next few days. It's the Grand Ole Opry and I didn't want to mess up. There would be 4,400 people in the audience, millions listening on the radio and dozens of Nashville's best musicians standing on the side of the stage waiting on me to make a mistake. I made up my mind that was not going to happen and it didn't. When I came off stage, somebody who knew it was my first time asked me what it was like. I said, "Well, I think I'll have to play it one more time because I don't remember anything that just happened."

The highs and lows of the music business sometimes happen fast and within a week of playing the Grand Ole Opry I was "let go." Why? I couldn't drive the bus and there was a road trip coming up and they found a bass player that could drive and hired him. I had heard stories of musicians being fired because they didn't fit in the band uniform, but I never thought I would lose a job because I couldn't drive a bus. Luckily, my wife was working a job in a souvenir shop, and that got us by. I got  busy trying to find a way to survive and hopefully learn how to drive a bus.

CHAPTER 15: LOUIS OWENS

After losing my first big-time gig in a mere 8 days, I was getting desperate for money. I got out the Yellow Pages (Google for phone numbers back then) and started calling every number that I could find associated with the music business. I got a lot of "Sorry, not hiring right now" answers but I finally got a call back from Louis Owens Productions. It was Louis Owens himself and after we chatted for a few minutes he invited me down to his Music Row office to meet and talk further. It was then I found out that Louis Owens was Dolly Parton's uncle. I think the fact that I didn't know who he was probably helped me in the interview since I wasn't trying to "use" him to get to Dolly. I think that was refreshing for him.

Louis and I talked for about an hour. Since I grew up in Appalachia and he grew up in East Tennessee there was sort of a mountain bond between us. When I told him about my experience with Stonewall Jackson and not being able to drive the bus, he laughed and said, "Welcome to Nashville."

Louis was one of those guys who was soft spoken, and you would never know he was such a key player in Nashville or how intelligent he was by the way he dressed and talked. He became my mentor and teacher, and he took me under his wing. He gave me great advice and kept me from making poor decisions and rookie mistakes. If I had questions, he always had answers and I admired the way he thought and handled business.

Louis was the first person to take t-shirts and merchandise sales on the road traveling with country artists. He started off being Ronnie Milsap's merchandise manager and introduced merchandise sales on a Milsap tour. Louis bought the equipment to print t-shirts, baseball caps and other tour souvenirs. He was so successful the first year that Milsap took the merchandise business away from him. Because of Louis's success, he negotiated deals with other artists to handle their merchandise sales and it became a booming business.

Louis bought his own bus and trailer and hired me to travel with him selling merchandise. He taught me the ins and outs of selling and, most importantly, he taught me how to drive a bus. We were doing a tour with Roy Clark and we were traveling to Valentine, Nebraska. It was late at night and the road was straight as far as you could see. He yelled for me to come up front and as we  were rolling down the road at 70 miles an hour he simply got up and stepped out of the driver's seat and said, "Slide in - you're driving." I said, "Louis, you know I've never driven a bus," and he said, "You have now." He spent about 15 minutes with me showing me all the gauges I needed to watch, what all the switches did and how to get off at an exit if it became necessary. Then he went to bed.

Of course, my job was just to keep it on the road and get the feel of what it was like to drive such a monster. It was surprising how much time it took to get it slowed down and how to take a curve or exit without throwing people out of their sleeper bunks. Maneuvering in and out of truck stops was another challenge, but he took his time, talked me through it all and I never lost another job because I couldn't drive a bus.

Louis lived next door to Dolly and we often printed and applied iron-on logos on t-shirts and baseball caps at his house. Occasionally Dolly would stop by. Louis's wife Colleen was a beautician and took care of Dolly's wigs and many of them were stored in Louis's basement. I don't recall ever seeing Dolly dressed up or wearing a wig when she'd come around. She was very plain looking with little or no makeup and very short hair without her wig. She would often wear a man's flannel shirt and a scarf on her head. I guess I'm one of a handful of people to meet her husband Carl Dean. I talked with Carl one day and asked him why he didn't come out on the road with us when we were selling Dolly's merchandise. He said, "The truth is I really don't care for her singing." I think he was joking but I wasn't quite sure.

A lot Dolly's fans knew Louis, so when we were selling merchandise on her tours, they would often ask to take a photo with him. The strangest thing would happen when Carl went on the road with us. Nobody recognized him. The fans would push him aside to get a photo with Louis.

Carl enjoyed fixing up old cars in the garage at Dolly's house and they had an old wood-paneled station wagon they would drive around Nashville so as not to be recognized. Dolly with her flannel shirt and headscarf and Carl just being himself.

My wife Judi became friends with Louis's wife and the next thing I know Dolly has asked my wife to come over and help take care of her house. They had a fun time, and I remember one time they were looking at a National Enquirer tabloid and commenting on the stories. It was funny because they believed a lot of the stories, but when they came across an article about Dolly they would laugh because they knew it wasn't true.

As with a lot of families who grew up in the mountains, they were clannish people. If they liked you and you were in their inner circle, they would do anything for you. When my father became gravely ill in 1983, I was on the road in Mobile, Alabama. I couldn't get a flight home so Louis and Dolly arranged a plane to get me to his bedside a few days before he passed away. That's an act of kindness I will never forget. Louis died in 2014 at the age of 80.

CHAPTER 16: LITTLE JIMMY DICKENS

W hen I wasn't on the road or working with Louis Owens, I spent at least three hours a day practicing. I had come out of a rock and disco band and needed some time to brush up on my country music. I had a cassette player/radio combination, and I would listen to WSM Radio and record the songs. If something came on that I didn't know, I had it on tape, and I'd rewind and play it until I got it right. I wanted to be ready if I got a call to play. It wasn't that I couldn't play country, but I didn't know that many of the newer songs. I didn't even know a lot of the language Nashville musicians used in describing how to play a certain style. I remember one time someone told me the song was a 4/4 shuffle and I didn't know what that meant. I had a lot of catching up to do, so I started learning everything I could.

I also sat down and wrote letters to three successful people in Nashville that grew up near my hometown in West Virginia. Those letters went to Grand Ole Opry star Little Jimmy Dickens; Musician's Hall of Fame member, Charlie McCoy; and steel guitarist, Russ Hicks. I had worked with Dickens' stepbrother at the coal mine and I included that in the letter in an attempt to impress him and let him know I was "home folk."

When my letter arrived at Dickens' house, he was doing a tour in California. On that tour he had caught his bass player and drummer smoking pot with the daughter of the local Sheriff, who was also the show promoter. Needless to say, he fired them both. Lucky for me, my letter arrived that same day. I got a call from his wife Mona asking if I would play a show the following week with them in Little Rock, Arkansas. Of course, I said yes and that excitement of my first experience at the Opry returned. It was a dream job for sure to be playing with Little

Jimmy Dickens.

The next day I got another call from Mona saying that Dickens had called another bass player he knew and they were sorry but it looked like the other bass player would be taking the job. Another "welcome to Nashville" moment for me. I sat around the house the next day very depressed and trying to figure out my next move.

The following day the phone rang, and it was Mona again saying the other bass player wasn't going to be able to take the job and they wanted me to be at their house on Friday night at 6 pm. It was a 48-hour notice. Trust me, I knew a few of his songs but I didn't know all of them and there were so many I wasn't sure what to work on for the show. I called Mona and she asked Dickens. He told her to tell me not to worry about it. We would go over everything on the trip to Arkansas. Well, I worried about it, so I got all the big hits down, but with some uncertainty about progressions and intros and outs. I didn't read charts at the time, so I was really taking a leap into deep water.

The night I arrived at the house it was dark and drizzling rain. We would be traveling in a custom van pulling an equipment trailer (Dickens always told people his bus was "in the bank"). I saw the other band members standing between the van and the equipment trailer and as I approached and said hello, I saw Little Jimmy Dickens laying on his back in the driveway messing with the lighting wires on the trailer. As I stepped up, the first words I heard him say was, "If anybody else gets down here and gets their hands dirty, they're fired." Obviously, a sarcastic referral that no one was helping him, but it was good to hear that he had a wit and sense of humor even during a bad situation.

Once everything was working, we took a few minutes in the kitchen to dry off and get warm. After that we got everything loaded and headed to Arkansas. It was about a 6-hour trip from Nashville and Dickens had an 8-track player in the van and an 8-track tape that contained his big hits. As we listened to each song, he, or one of the band members would say, "That's not exactly how we'll be doing it, but you'll get it." Again, another "Welcome to Nashville" moment where most musicians know every song and can cover any major blunders. At that point, I was not that Nashville musician and I knew it. My stress level probably doubled as song after song came and went with the other band members encouraging me, "Don't worry about it, you'll get it."

The next day it's time for soundcheck. I'm dreading it because I know I'm not ready to be here, but I wanted it so badly I was going to fake my way through it somehow. Luckily at soundcheck we only did a couple of songs and they were ones that I knew so everyone was saying, "There you go. You're gonna be fine."

Other than playing one song on the Grand Ole Opry, I had never been in front of a crowd of more than a few hundred people. Most of those crowds I had played for were people there to party, so the band was rarely the main focus of their attention. That was about to change. We got to the venue and there were several thousand people. They were all sitting there looking at the stage waiting on Little Jimmy Dickens. I had never been in the spotlight like this and, for the next 60 minutes, I was sweating, shaking and cursing myself for every mistake I made. I kept saying to myself, "I'm playing with Little Jimmy Dickens" and I would look over and there he was standing just a few feet from me - Little Jimmy Dickens!

After the show I was amazed at people asking me for my autograph. A few weeks earlier, I had been in a bar in Stillwater, Oklahoma, and now people want my autograph. It's the perception that if you're playing with a star, you are elevated to a high level of worthiness as a musician.

I don't remember much about that show except that I made

a lot of mistakes and I felt like I would get a phone call that I was fired when we got back. That call never came and our next show was the Grand Ole Opry. I spent hours working on songs for that Opry spot. It would only be two or three songs at the most, but I wanted to be rock solid. No matter what he decided to do I would be ready. There would be no rehearsal during the week and Dickens wouldn't tell you what he was going to do until about 30 minutes before going on stage. We would run through those songs so we could all warmup and then head to the stage.

As I got to the stage, I noticed the stage was a lot brighter than my earlier visit with Stonewall Jackson. The drummer told me it was lit up because our portion of the Opry would be on live national TV. Even though I was ready this time, the term "national TV" added another level of stress to my evening. Now it's not just the live audience of 4,400 people, a radio audience of several million, and the best musicians in the world on the side of the stage watching. Now we have lights, cameras and a national TV audience of millions. Again, I don't remember much about that appearance except I kept hearing "smile and move" in my head from my show band days and cameras being wheeled shoved in my face. It was another experience I got under my belt and another goal accomplished.

My most memorable Little Jimmy Dickens' story happened on my second road trip out with him. It was a chilly day as we traveled to the outskirts of Washington, D.C., for a show at a military base in Virginia. We got into town in the late evening the day before the show and settled into three rooms at a roadside motel. It was a one-level, L-shaped motel, and there were probably 30 rooms total. It wasn't a fancy place, but a welcome site when you're beat-up from traveling all day in custom van. I figure that van felt like a bus to Dickens who was 4'11" tall. At any rate, we settled in for a good night's rest. I was rooming with drummer Ralph Kinnen, and we both turned in early looking forward to having the night off with nothing to do but rest -- a night to catch up. Even though we were in Virginia and several miles from Washington, D.C., you could hear sirens occasionally wailing throughout the night. I slept well and didn't really hear much once I went to sleep. At about 4 am, I was awakened by a siren that sounded like it was right outside my room. As I awoke, I could see flashing red lights bouncing off the blinds in the window and the lights were stationary, not typical of fast-moving emergency vehicles. When I realized the flashing lights were right outside my room, I jumped to my feet and peeled back the curtain revealing a parking lot full of fire trucks, ambulances and police cars. Oh my God, the motel was on fire!!!

I rousted Ralph from his sleep and quickly jumped into my pants to warn Dickens and the other band members, guitarist David Nye and steel guitarist Jimmy Hodge, of the impending crisis. I was the new guy in the band at the time and I felt like this would score some big points for me. I could see the headlines "Band Member Saves Little Jimmy Dickens From Fire." In the L-shaped configuration of the motel, our room was the closest to the fire, just to our left. Dickens was in the room immediately to my right.

I banged on his door with all my might and yelled his name. I could just see it - "McVey Saves Grand Ole Opry Star." As Dickens groggily opened the door he said, "What is it?" I said, "Jim, the motel is on fire!" In his many years of being on the road I'm sure Little Jimmy Dickens had seen everything, but his reply shocked me. He leaned out the door, looked to the left, saw the fire and calmly said, "Wake me up when it gets to your room." He closed the door and went back to bed, seeming perturbed I had awakened him for such a trivial thing. I thought I was going to be a hero and guarantee my job for life. Neither happened. The fire was extinguished well before it got close to our rooms. The following day it was back to business as usual, but I will never forget that day when I almost became a hero.

There were many stories and experiences associated with my time with Dickens. Sometimes on a late-night run I would be driving, and he would be sitting in the passenger seat. The band would be asleep, and we would talk about everything from his time with Hank Williams, Roy Acuff, and other stars to growing up in West Virginia, especially Beckley near where we both grew up and had some mutual acquaintances. He would talk about his family and how poor they were growing up. As he relived those times, I would often see tears in his eyes. He loved the people of West Virginia and would get emotional talking about them, especially the people who sacrificed so he could pursue his music career.

He told me a story about A. A. Farmer, a man we both knew. "Mr. Farmer" as Dickens referred to him, owned a store in Dickens' hometown of Bolt, West Virginia. Farmer had money, drove a nice Cadillac, and lived in a beautiful home.

When Dickens was just starting out, he would hitchhike about 20 miles every morning from Bolt to Beckley to sign on the local radio station WJLS. A part of Dickens' duties at the station was to crow like a rooster when the station signed on. Occasionally Mr. Farmer would make an early morning run to Beckley and pass Dickens on the side of the road hitchhiking. Dickens told me it made him so mad that Mr. Farmer knew him and wouldn't pick him up. When Dickens got famous and bought his first Cadillac, he drove it to Bolt and right up Mr. Farmer's driveway into his yard and right up to his front door and blew the horn. He said Mr. Farmer came out and spent some time with him and they patched things up. Mr. Farmer apologized for leaving him standing on the side of the road on more than a few occasions.

It was no secret back then that Dickens enjoyed taking a drink or two and there are several stories that were the result of that. If we were on a road trip, he would sit in the passenger seat and would drink until he would drift off to sleep. If you were driving during one of those occasions, it could be a great experience or a nightmare. If he had a drink, he was notorious for taking the opposite side of any argument that came up and if that didn't happen, he would create one.

This brings me to the story many of my friends have heard me tell concerning my "swimming trunks" incident at the Opry. It was a hot summer's day over 100 degrees and I wore shorts and a t-shirt to the Opry. It wasn't unusual, since most musicians did it, but I just picked a bad day to do it. I would change into my stage clothes before performing so I didn't see the big deal in what I wore backstage since no one saw me but the people backstage. We did our spot on the Grand Ole Opry and then headed to Michigan for a road show the next day.

Dickens had a very serious arthritic neck issue where the vertebra in his neck restricted him from turning his head without turning his whole body. In the van, he never made an attempt to turn and look at you when he talked to you. If you were driving, he would reach over and hit you on the shoulder with the back of his hand and ask, "Are you listening?"

This trip started off fine and we all got a chuckle when Dickens pointed at the sign in front of the Nashville Palace that read "Tonight Jeannie Seely (and underneath) All you can eat $5.95."

Our drummer, Tom Holland had introduced a drink to Dickens called a "Snowshoe." I don't know what was in it, but I think it was a cocktail of Peppermint Schnapps and Wild Turkey. It was a favorite with Dickens and when he wanted a drink he would start yelling "Shoe" which was Tom's cue to serve one up.

So, I was driving the first shift out of Nashville and Dickens started yelling "Shoe!" I was starting to get a bad feeling since this is usually the beginning of a long evening for the victim of his wrath. Since I was driving, it was most likely going to be me.

He started off by asking me, "Why did you wear swimming trunks to the Grand Ole Opry - the Mother Church of Country Music?" Hoping to head this off right then and there, I said, "Jim that was shorts and I wore them because it was really hot today." He said, "I know swimming trunks when I see them and that was swimming trunks." I thought I won't respond and maybe he will drop it. He did not. Instead, he hit me on the shoulder and said, "Are you listening? I said I know swimming trunks when I see them." Again, I tried to ease out of it by saying, "Jim those were just shorts." Almost before I was finished, he started yelling, "I know swimming trunks when I see them and they were still wet!" Again, I tried the silent treatment, but he wouldn't let it end there. "If you ever wear swimming trunks to the Grand Ole Opry again, you're fired." I didn't respond. I got another slap to the shoulder, "Are you listening?" he asked. I replied, "Yes sir, that won't ever happen again and I'm sorry."

There was silence for about the next 10 minutes. None of the other band members would talk during these times because they knew they could be the next victim. So, there was silence and then he reached over and tapped me on the shoulder and asked, "Did you hear me when I told you not to wear your swimming trunks to the Grand Ole Opry?" I said, "Yes, sir." And then he started making remarks every so often to remind of this cardinal sin I had committed. He mumbled something about "I can't believe anybody would wear their swimming trunks to the Grand Ole Opry." And to top it off, he would ask the other band members what they thought, and they knew to agree with him or else.

The biggest drinking disaster story happened on his 62nd birthday, December 20, 1982. Dickens agent, Smiley Wilson had booked several shows up and down the east coast going as far north as North Yarmouth, Maine. The problems began when all the dates fell out, except for the one in Maine. Dickens didn't want to go. It was his birthday, and it was an 18-hour drive in the van to get there. It was cold and it snowed off and on during the trip. When we got to the venue, the first thing the show promoter did was give Dickens a fifth of Jack Daniels whiskey for his birthday. We all knew then it was going to be a long night. We had to do two shows that night and the first went well. Dickens had just enough to drink to make the show lively and funny and he just killed the crowd as he often did. After the first show, they had a birthday cake, and it was announced it was his birthday, so people started buying him drinks.

We all went on stage for the second show and we did a couple of songs and introduced him. He was a mess. He barely made it on stage. He was slurring his words, repeating the same jokes and he was just incoherent. We did his big hit, "We Could" and he told a joke or two and then turned to me and said, "We Could."

I said, "Jim we just did that," and he got angry and yelled," Dammit I said, 'We Could'." So, we played it a second time.

At this point the promoter's wife came to the stage and said to me, "Get him off the stage." I was so angry that I told her, "You got him drunk, you get him off." She walked away and went over to two policemen and they started walking toward the stage. I didn't want it to end like that so I told Tom, "play him off," meaning do the end of the show song so he would know to leave. As he got off stage one of the officers respectfully helped him to the dressing room.

As we were tearing down our equipment, I told the band I was going to go check on him. When I opened the door, he was sitting on the floor trying to put on his pants and assured me he was fine. But they wanted us out of the building as soon as possible so I went back to the stage. A little later our steel guitar player, Jimmy Hodge said he would go check on him and when he came back to the stage he was laughing. We asked him what happened, and he said Dickens was still in the floor putting his pants on when Hodge unknowingly asked, "Where's that asshole that asked you to get out of the building?" Standing behind the door was the policeman who had escorted Dickens to the dressing room and Dickens pointed to him and answered, "That nice gentleman standing over there."

Dickens' wife, Mona had bought him a beautiful black full-length overcoat for this birthday, and since she knew this was going to be a long cold trip, she gave it to him before we left. It looked like it was cashmere. It was gorgeous. Behind the venue where we parked the van and trailer there was about four feet of snow piled up on each side of the  driveway and the van and trailer were both covered in road salt used to clear the icy roads. There was probably 18 inches of walking space beside the van and trailer, so our next challenge was to get Dickens in the van without him getting that coat covered in salt residue. We failed. I think he wiped the entire distance from the back of the trailer to the van door covering this coat with salt and road grime.

I was conjuring up in my mind the scene when we got back home and Mona flipping out over the condition of that coat. She would always implore us when we left on a road trip to do everything we could to keep him from drinking. I knew she would kill us, but this time there was nothing we could have done.

The next day, Dickens got in his normal spot on the passenger side and was quiet as a mouse on the trip home. He never said a word, but that was typical behavior when he knew he had messed up. I knew he was embarrassed so I thought I'd break the ice and said, "Man Jim, 62 came in like lion." He just smiled but never said a word until he saw a McDonalds sign. He loved the McDonalds coffee because he said it was "always fresh" unlike some truck stop coffee. If he wanted to stop at McDonalds he would simply yell, "Arches" letting us know he had seen the Golden Arches sign at an upcoming exit.

For the most part the band kept Dickens' drinking under control and I only saw it affect a couple of his shows. When we would get into a town the night before a show, he would always tell whoever was driving to stop at a liquor store. If I was driving and saw a liquor store, I would always look in the opposite direction and hope it didn't catch his eye. Or I would purposely direct his attention to something else so he wouldn't see it. If he spotted a liquor store it reminded me of a kid seeing a Dairy Queen. He'd call your name and point toward the sign, but I always acted like I didn't see it or was going too fast to stop. One night, having passed up three liquor stores, I had pushed my luck a little too far. He said, "Dick, if you pass one more liquor store, you're fired."

Dickens used the word "fired" a lot, but one night we finally got an idea of what he really meant. He called us all into the dressing room before the show and we knew something was up because he had never done that before. As we entered, he proclaimed, "If I fire you all tonight, you're all hired back tomorrow." If he was drinking, I think he was afraid he would fire us all and wouldn't have time to rehire us.

Some of the trips were long and the van was customized inside with a bunk built to fit Dickens' 4'11" frame. He could stretch out quite comfortably and he seemed to be able to sleep soundly on the interstates. In the back of the van was a bed that could sleep two and then there were the two seats up front. Where they had modified the van and removed two seats, they had not replaced a bolt in the floorboard, and you could actually see the road if you pulled back the shag carpet. Under Dickens' bunk we kept extra oil, brake fluid, a funnel and other things you might need on a road trip. David Nye discovered that the funnel would fit the hole in the floorboard, thereby eliminating him having to wait for an official stop if he had to pee. I'm not sure the cars behind us appreciated his ingenuity.

David, who also enjoyed taking a drink, kept little flasks in his guitar case, in his show boots, and anywhere else he could find a nook. Those flasks came in handy at times when Dickens would become irate about not stopping at the liquor store.

Dickens was as quick-witted as they come and here's an example of that. I had never been out West, and we were doing a show in Arizona and there were a lot of Native Americans in the crowd. Dickens sent word for me to come to the dressing room where he very seriously said, "Dick, I just wanted you to know that tonight, don't do Kawliga." It was a reference to the Hank Williams song about a wooden Indian in a cigar store.

We were traveling during a time when there were gas shortages. We made it a rule that when the van would get to half a tank, we would start looking for a gas station. One night when Jimmy Hodge was driving, he ran out of gas. Instead of being too concerned, he climbed into the back bunk and went to sleep. I woke up cold and when I questioned why we were sitting on the side of the road Hodge replied we had run out of gas. Tom got up and he and I started hitchhiking to the nearest gas station where we got gas. The guy who picked us up was nice enough to wait and drive us back to the van so we could get back underway.

We almost had a similar problem when we traveled through the Grand Teton Mountains. We were almost empty when we found a gas station that had closed for the night and spent the night in the parking lot until they opened the next morning.

We traveled about 200 days that year, and one trip was extraordinary in many ways. We had played just outside of Philadelphia, Pennsylvania, and our next show was in Washington state. Dickens flew to Washington, but we drove, and it was memorable. It took us 72 hours. No rooms, no showers, no home-cooked meals, but boy did we see some sights. When we got out West, we decided to go through the Teton Mountains, and they were beautiful.

From there we spent a day in Yellowstone Park where we witnessed "Old Faithful", the hot springs and lots of wildlife. On some of the roads the snow was piled up 10 feet and moose would get in the road, couldn't get off, and would trot in front of us. One time there were two moose cows and a bull in front of us and we got a little too close. The bull stopped and Tom got out to take a picture and it charged us, pulling up just short of hitting us. At about that same time a game warden pulled in behind us, beeped his siren, got on his P.A. system and told us to stay put until the moose had a chance to get out of sight. There was a side road ahead and they were able to get off the road and back into the wooded area.

The smallest crowd I ever experienced with Dickens was on this tour. We were playing somewhere in Washington and the promoter hadn't done a very good job. There were 14 people in the building. Dickens was a true professional and he came out and the first thing he said was, "Ladies and gentlemen, I notice we have a small crowd here tonight but it's not the smallest crowd I've had. Once I came on stage and there was one man in the audience. I told him that it didn't bother me in the least and he would be getting our full and complete show and I would be leaving nothing out. The man said, 'Hurry up shorty, I'm the janitor and I'd like to get home.'" It was interesting because with a crowd that small, the show becomes more personal for those who attend and, honestly, it was a lot of fun.

After two weeks in Washington and Oregon, it was time to head to the next show, which happened to be all the way across the United States in Columbia, South Carolina. We dropped off Dickens at the airport and we drove 68 hours back across the U.S. There would be no sightseeing on this trip and when we finished the show in South Carolina, we drove back to Nashville. I remember being so tired I didn't care if I lived or died.

When Jimmy Hodge left the band, Dickens hired Teddy Carr, a 20-year-old kid who was a remarkable steel guitarist player for his age. I made Teddy's first night playing on the Opry stage a memorable one. We were on Roy Acuff's portion of the show and I told Mr. Acuff it was Teddy's first night. Mr. Acuff would often stay on stage after he introduced an act and when it came time for Teddy's steel solo, Mr. Acuff stuck a legal pad in front of Teddy so he couldn't see his fretboard. Mr. Acuff only kept it there for a second, but you should have seen the panic on Teddy's face.

A month or so later, Dickens invited world-renowned steel guitarist and former Dickens band member, Buddy Emmons to play with us at the Opry. Teddy asked Dickens what he should do and Dickens replied, "Flog and log," meaning play something and log your time. Dickens joked, "If I were you, I'd just watch and learn because you wouldn't make a good wart on Emmons' ass."

Teddy got the job playing for Jack Greene and he made the mistake of telling Dickens as we were leaving on a road trip. Dickens had a few drinks and it was an unmerciful trip for young Teddy.

Following Teddy, Tom Holland had recommended a steel player named Richard Marz for the job. Richard was a great musician from New England. His real name was Richard Marzialo and he had worked with several major artists, but he never got along with Dickens. Richard was very outspoken and was continually bringing up subjects that prompted confrontations. He would bring a newspaper with him to read on the road and he would read certain articles to us and then state his opinion. This played perfectly into Dicken's hands where he usually took the opposite side of any argument and he and Dickens would go at each other. One night it went too far. Nobody seemed to push Dickens' buttons like Richard, and he wouldn't back off and let it simmer and go away. This night it nearly got physical.

Richard had read us an article about a Supreme Court judge and then gave his opinion on this judge. Dickens took the opposing view, and it was on. They yelled at each other for about half an hour until Dickens said, "Stop the van."

Dickens looked at Tom Holland and ordered Tom to "whip Richard's ass." Tom was shocked and started stuttering and trying to find a way to get things settled down. He said, "Now Jim, you know you don't want me to do that. Let's just think about all this." Dickens replied, "I want him out of this van so the next town we get to I want to take him to the bus station and get him a ticket home." Tom again tried to get control and pulled Dickens off to the side and told him, "We really need Richard for this show and when we get home, I'll find somebody else." Dickens relented but said, "OK, but next time don't hire anybody from north of Hendersonville," referring to a town about 20 miles north of Nashville. "No more Yankees," he added.

When we got home from that trip, the search was on for a new steel guitarist and Tom spent quite a bit of time choosing the replacement. He hired Tommy Phillips, a mild-mannered nice guy, who was the perfect person for the gig. A great musician with a quiet demeanor and didn't seem to be anyone that would be a problem. We all loved Tommy and Dickens would often introduce him jokingly, saying, "They came out with a Tommy Phillips bumper sticker today – it was blank." Another one was, "Tommy was so lazy he married a woman that already had two children." And to top it off he would say, "When

Tommy wakes up in the morning and says good morning, he's told you all he knows."

On one of our first road trips out with Tommy we played an outdoor show in Michigan. My stomach had been rumbling so as we got to the stage in front of the grandstand, I started looking for the nearest bathroom, just in case. Tommy said he saw a door under the stage that looked like it might be a dressing room. I asked one of the local guys helping us unload and he confirmed the dressing rooms were under the stage and there were bathrooms.

We started setting up for soundcheck and I felt like I had pushed the stomach issue to its limit. It was time to go to the bathroom. I walked around the stage to the dressing room door, and it was locked. I didn't panic because I figured the guy who helped us load in would have a key. He did not. But he did point out a camping area about two football fields away that had a bathhouse and restrooms.

I started walking. Each step I took told me this was going to be a close call. Just as I entered the bathroom, it let go. Fortunately, there were stalls there and I didn't see anyone else when I entered. I managed to get my pants off before any damage was done, but the underwear was a total loss. It took me 15 minutes to clean up and dispose of the underwear. When I got back to the stage everybody knew what happened because it took me so long. To this day, I not only find the nearest bathroom, but I also take time to make sure it's unlocked.

Dickens lived in Brentwood, Tennessee, about 10 miles south of Nashville. He had a nice home, with a well-groomed lawn and a nice driveway that went up a slight hill to the house. There was no gate in front of the home back then and toward the end of his shows he would always announce, "Ladies and gentlemen, it has been my sincere pleasure to entertain you tonight and if you ever come to Nashville and come to my home, you'll find no security guard, you'll find no gate and if you come up the driveway to my home you will always be welcome." It endeared him to his fans.

At the entrance to Dickens' driveway there were two columns on each side of the driveway. At the top of each column there were huge pots where you could plant small trees or shrubs. Several times in our travels Dickens had remarked that trees or shrubs he would see at homes or businesses would be perfect for his driveway pots. One such instance was at a hotel. At the hotel entrance were two well-groomed pine trees that Dickens thought would be perfect for this home. The next morning when we checked out and put our suitcases in the trailer, those two trees were in the trailer ready for the trip to Tennessee. To this day I don't know who it did, but Dickens was right, and those trees were perfect for his driveway pots. They were also a big hit with his wife, Mona.

For some reason we put music stars on a pedestal and rarely think of them doing normal things like we do. If it's something hard, they just hire someone to do it for them. But in the case of cleaning out a garage, it's likely a hired person may throw away something that had value.

I had seen the inside Dickens' garage on several occasions when we'd meet at his house to go on road trips. I had noticed old records in boxes and other discarded items, so when he said he was going to clean out the garage, I offered to help. It was a nice day and as we rummaged through things, I could tell he was getting tired of the task. So, it ended up with me opening boxes and showing him what was there, and he would decide to keep it or throw it away. In the case of the 33-rpm and 45 rpm records, there were hundreds. He didn't want them, so I boxed them up to take them home. Unfortunately, over the course of me moving four or five times over the years they have gotten lost or trashed.

He also gave me a hatband that was made from the fur of a baby seal. The killing of baby seals had become such a "hot button" issue that he couldn't take a chance on wearing it any longer. I wore it a few times on a cowboy hat that I had but decided it was not the right thing to do and stored it away.

As we continued the search and trash mission, I saw an old

brown case and I pulled it out and opened it. It was an old tape recorder. I said, "Jim, what's the story on this old tape recorder?" He casually said, "Hank Williams gave me that." That meant it had been around for 33 years or more. I asked where he wanted me to put it and his answer amazed me. "Just throw it in the trash," he said. I thought he was joking but he was serious. I told him I was going to keep it and he told me that would be fine. As I'm driving home that evening, I am wondering if Hank Williams may have recorded some of his songs with that recorder. The possibilities were endless.

I really felt like I needed to take this tape recorder, that I considered a historic piece, to the Country Music Hall Of Fame and I did. I told them the story and, even though I have never seen it displayed, I know they have thousands of items in their archives and I am sure it's where it belongs. I assumed they would contact Dickens to get the story that went with it, but I never heard any more about it.

My time with Little Jimmy Dickens was probably the most exciting time in my life. When I wasn't on the road with him, I was selling t-shirts with Louis Owens and hanging out with stars like Dolly Parton, Merle Haggard and Barbara Mandrell. I learned a lot.

CHAPTER 17: MERLE HAGGARD

T hen came the news that Merle Haggard had asked Little Jimmy Dickens to open some shows for him. Those shows were some of the most memorable of my life and the most lucrative. Louis Owens happened to be handling Merle Haggard's merchandise, so I was getting paid to play bass for Little Jimmy Dickens, opening the Haggard shows, and selling t-shirts and merchandise when I came off stage. Ironically, I made more money selling Haggard merchandise than I did playing. This was in 1982-83 at the height of the "Urban Cowboy" craze and Haggard was drawing record numbers of young people to his shows. In fact, there were nights when an IRS Agent would be waiting to count the money and make sure they got their tax dollars on site. Artist merchandise was a lucrative business, and the IRS knew it.

One of the most interesting things that happened during the Merle Haggard tour happened in Louisville, Kentucky. In certain cities there are powerful unions for stagehands and crews, and Louisville is one of those cities. The stagehands have lots of say in how equipment is loaded in and how things get done in a union venue on a show day.

Haggard was working on a new album and typically after he did his sound check for the sound engineers, he and the band would work on new songs in preparation to record them. Haggard was one of the few artists who still used his road band in the recording studio. That was the case on this day.

I was standing at the side of the stage when I saw Haggard's road manager Fuzzy Owens talking to the stagehands' union representative. After a brief chat, Fuzzy walked on stage and told Haggard the stagehands wanted to take their dinner break and requested a "dark stage." A dark stage meant all activity on stage would cease.

Haggard told Fuzzy that he would really like to continue to work with the band and if the stagehands wanted to go to dinner, he would pay them extra if they would let him rehearse. Haggard asked if they could leave the sound system turned on while they were gone.

Fuzzy approached the union rep and explained that they were scheduled to record the following week and Haggard wanted to go over some of the new songs. The union rep vehemently rejected the offer and demanded a "dark stage" while they were gone to eat. Fuzzy went back to Haggard and told him they had rejected his offer, to which Haggard said, "If they want a dark stage, they can have a dark stage all night. Pack it up boys we're not doing a show here tonight."

It was several hours before the show but there were fans already lined up at the front door and when they were informed the show was cancelled, they were not happy. Fortunately, we all got out of there before there was any confrontation and drove across the river to Jeffersonville, Indiana, where we had rooms for the night.

When we arrived one of Haggard's band members informed me Emmylou Harris was in town and she was coming up to Haggard's suite and they were going to have a "guitar pull" where everybody would sit around the room with an acoustic guitar and play their newly written songs. Haggard had invited Little Jimmy Dickens to the get together and, of course, I was trying to figure out a way to get in that room too. Haggard agreed to let us come in and hang out. I found a spot in the corner and sat on the floor. The suite was spacious with a huge living room and a long sectional couch. There sat Emmylou, Haggard, Leona Williams and a couple of Haggard's and Emmylou's band members. It was a surreal scene, and I had a feeling I was witnessing history.

At one point, Haggard looked at Dickens and asked him if he had written any songs and Dickens replied that he had. Haggard asked if he would do one, and Dickens seemed a little intimidated, which was unlike Dickens, who would jump into most any situation with full confidence. But this was Merle Haggard, one of the greatest country music songwriters of all time. After everyone encouraged him, Dickens picked up his guitar and sang a song he had written called "Shopping For Dresses." The room erupted into applause and Haggard immediately asked Dickens to step into another room, and there he asked Dickens if he could record the song.

Being around Dickens for the next few days was incredible. It may have been the happiest and most excited I ever saw him. The song ended up on Haggard's album "Going Where The Lonely Go". I think Haggard ended up changing the second verse and took credit as half writer. Haggard also claimed the song's publishing portion, which gave Haggard 75% ownership of the song. It's not unusual for a deal to happen that way in Nashville and Dickens seemed fine with that outcome. When I asked him about it, he said, "25% of something is better than 100% of nothing. And ... Merle Haggard wants to record my song."

Nearly every day after that night, Dickens talked to Haggard about writing songs. Dickens really wanted to write a song with Haggard. We knew Haggard was writing songs almost every night after the shows on the bus enroute to the next show. It was more than evident that Dickens wanted to ride the bus with Haggard one night and write with him. I know Haggard loved Dickens and I know Haggard loved to write songs, but I'm not sure he was excited about Dickens being on the bus with him. But, one night Haggard agreed, and Dickens climbed on his bus, guitar in hand. These were happy days for Dickens.

We all wondered what the next day would bring and I happened to be standing by the bus when they emerged. Dickens was excited and energized and he said, "Let me off this song factory," indicating he felt it had been a successful night. A few minutes later Haggard came off the bus and he put his arm around my neck and said, "Walk with me." As we walked Haggard said jokingly, "Don't ever let that little son-of-a-bitch on my bus again." We had a good laugh and I asked Haggard how it went. He said simply, "It was a long night."

One of the most amazing shows we did with Haggard was

a private party on a cattle ranch near Odessa, Texas. Wealthy rancher Clayton Williams had created a breed of cattle known as "Brangus." Each year he would have a cattle auction at his 27,000-acre ranch called "Happy Cove." The ranch was beautifully groomed and had an airstrip capable of handling private jets and the driveway to his house was miles long. The auction was an "invitation only" event, and more than 3,000 people attended.

Clayton had hired seven bands covering any musical taste a guest might have. There were rock bands, jazz bands, country bands, Mariachi bands, and Merle Haggard as the evening's finale. It was sweltering and the Dickens boys strolled around listening to the bands, trying the many different foods that were offered. I can remember them doing French fries in a 55-gallon drum. There was lots of beer and other spirits and no shortage of drinkers.

Airplanes were constantly flying over and landing. Some showboat pilots were flying their private planes recklessly over the event and doing stunts that I knew to be illegal. I fully expected a disaster at any time.

There were hundreds of custom buses and motorhomes and you could tell these people were super wealthy. The ladies were dressed in tailored outfits and the men were wearing boots worth thousands. It was unbelievable in many ways, and by the time Haggard took the stage there were lots of people ready to party. It was a great show.

The Haggard shows were tremendous, and the Haggard team treated us first class. We got a hot meal catered before every show and Haggard had a chiropractor on the road that would crack your neck and back if you needed it. When we arrived at a show, I would set my bass, still in the case, on the side of the stage. When I went on stage it was there on a stand; it had been tuned; the amp set to my specs; and all I had to do was pick it up and play. After the show I would set it on the stand, and it would be packed and, in my case, and placed on the side of the stage for load out.

The crowds were huge and there were shows where I got to be the guinea pig for the sound crew to check things out and I got to sing the first song to open the show. I then had the privilege of introducing Dickens. Another perk in traveling with Haggard was he was married to Leona Williams at the time. It was so cool hanging out on the side of the stage as she opened his portion of the show and off stage watching her craft songs like "You Take Me For Granted" that would become hits. She was a beautiful lady and person.

The show would start with Little Jimmy Dickens doing about 30 minutes; Haggard's band did a couple of songs; Leona did a few songs and then sang "That's The Way Love Goes". There was no introduction for Haggard. During Norm Hamlett's steel guitar solo Haggard would simply stroll on stage and sing the last chorus and the crowds would go wild. Every night when Haggard did that it gave me chill bumps. It got to the point where I would challenge myself by saying, "I'm not gonna let that happen tonight." It always did.

One day I was visiting with Haggard's band on their bus when Haggard stepped on board. In the cup holders on the bus there was cocaine stored in canisters meant for 35mm camera film and there were always baggies of marijuana. Haggard announced, "Boys you are smoking way too much pot. I don't mind you smoking it but once you get high you need to stop." Once he left everybody laughed, but he was dead serious about it.

Nearly every night after a show there would be a party or a lot of us would end up at a local club where we got the royal treatment. We were living the dream. After an all-night party I was walking into our hotel around 6 am and I glanced over at the restaurant. There sat Haggard by himself. At that time, he had grown a beard and was wearing a little hat and people didn't recognize him. I don't know if he had been up all night or if he was just coming down for breakfast, but I went over and asked if I could join him. It was another one of those "pinch myself" moments because I'm sitting across the table from Merle Haggard.

Just Haggard and me.

One of the things I liked to do when I would get one-on-one with a major artist like that was to talk about the music business. I wanted to learn. I found out that he had the shows taped every night and he would listen and critique the shows on the way to the next gig. He told me some things he thought we could do to make Dickens' show better. He told me he considered the bass player one of the most important musicians in the band. It was a melodic instrument and had percussive value since it worked so closely with the kick drum. I was skeptical that he listened to the shows, but he brought to my attention several specific places where I knew there were problems. It amazed me. Every morning I would go down early to see if he was there and I was lucky enough to sit with him a few times. Despite his issues with drugs and alcohol he was a brilliant man and impressed me with his knowledge and insight. As the Haggard tour came to an end, I realized just how much I had learned from the experience and what it was like to tour the country in "superstar" fashion.

It was also good to share the stage with his band members, most of whom are legendary musicians. Roy Nichols (Guitar), Tiny Moore (Mandolin and Fiddle), Norm Hamlet (Steel Guitar), Jimmy Belkin (Fiddle), Don Markham (Saxophone), Mark Yeary (Piano), Biff Adams (Drums), and Dennis Hromek (Bass).

With the end of the Haggard tour, it was back to doing the Grand Ole Opry and individual road shows with Dickens. Then one day, Tom Holland brought to my attention that Calvin Crawford, a bass player and one of Dickens best friends and hunting and fishing buddy, was losing his job with singer David Houston. Houston had decided to move back to his home state of Louisiana and was going to be dropping his Nashville band. Houston played the Opry often, so I had gotten to know Calvin, and I also knew that Calvin and Dickens were close and had been for many years before I came on the scene. I may have been wrong, but I sensed that Dickens was going to hire Calvin when Houston left town. So, I started looking around for a new job. I wanted to quit rather than taking the chance of being "let go." I wanted to be a step ahead of Dickens making that choice.

I told Dickens' drummer that I would be leaving, and he let Dickens know. Sure enough, Calvin became the bass player and he and I remained friends until his death in 1999. I never really had the right to be upset with Calvin and, since we both lived in Hendersonville, Tennessee, we crossed paths every now and then. The last time I saw him was after I rear-ended him coming out of the bank. I was fumbling with some papers and bam - hit him in the back. I was so happy and sad at the same time. Happy it was him and knowing he wasn't going to sue me, and sad it happened and was my fault.

I was always looking for situations to make money and most artists were paying musicians on a per show basis. That's great when you are working a lot, especially during the summer months, but the winter months were often long and lean. One time I was complaining to Dickens about not making a lot of money during the winter and he asked me, "What did you do with all that money you made last summer?" I answered, "I bought back everything I sold last winter." He appreciated my quick answer and laughed, but never asked me again.

I had such a great time with Dickens and the band, and I am forever thankful he gave me the chance to get that experience and knowledge with a true legend in country music.

CHAPTER 18: NAT STUCKEY

Before leaving Little Jimmy Dickens, I had put on an intense search for another artist gig. Someone told me Nat Stuckey was looking for a road band and when I contacted him, he hired me to put together a band. I now felt comfortable that my transition from one job to another would be smooth and it would eliminate any money worries.

Nat was a well-known songwriter who had written the big Jim Ed Brown hit, "Pop A Top" later recorded by Alan Jackson. Nat had top ten hits of his own, including "Has Anybody Seen My Sweet Thang," "Plastic Saddle," and "Don't Pay The Ransom." He was a wonderful man and entertainer. While he wasn't superstar status, he was well respected and was still in demand.

I put together a band of "rookies" to the Nashville music scene and brought in musicians from all over the country. Drummer Phil Fisher from Texas, keyboard player Jesse Terrell from Alabama and guitarist Randy James from Arizona. None of them had ever played with a major artist or knew how things were done in Nashville. By that, I mean there would rarely be a rehearsal. Bands would listen to the songs and learn them like the records and a lot of times the first time you saw the artist was when he or she walked on stage.

Since I was in charge of this band, I made sure we rehearsed Nat's show until we had it down to perfection. We rehearsed at the Musician's Union, where they had a nice stage, and it was free to use for union members. During one of our final rehearsals for Nat, an RCA representative came by and, after hearing us, wanted to know if we would be interested in playing some dates with Tommy St. John, a new artist they had just signed. I negotiated a deal with RCA and for several months we were able to do both jobs.

Our first show with Nat Stuckey was opening for Tammy

Wynette. Remember, none of the other musicians had ever played with an artist and had never played in a superstar concert situation. To say they were scared to death is an understatement. I was doing everything I could to reassure them that we were ready, rehearsed, and hey, what could go wrong? I implored them, "Let's get out there and have fun."

The show was sold out. Thousands of people. The stage was huge, and the lighting and sound system was massive. As I walked out and plugged in, I noticed they all were sporting nervous smiles, obviously intimidated by the crowd and surroundings. I was nervous, but more for them than me, remembering what it was like to walk on the huge stages with Haggard. The emcee introduced Nat and the show was on. It was an incredible experience, especially for the other guys who had never played any show of this magnitude. The show was flawless, and we played every song to perfection. As the show went on, you could see and feel their confidence building. Nat had the crowd in the palm of his hand, and he left the stage to thunderous applause. We all sighed a breath of relief and started unplugging to leave the stage. Then something happened that we never expected. - the emcee called Nat back out to the stage for an encore.

We had played all Nat's songs we had rehearsed, and we hadn't thought about or rehearsed an encore song. I looked around at the other musicians, seeing their faces go from relief to panic. I was very uneasy myself but trying not to show it. Would he repeat a song we knew, or would he pull something out of his hat that we didn't know? Jesse kept asking, "What is he going to do?" and all I could do was shrug my shoulders. I saw a nervous smile on Randy's face, and Phil was looking down, shaking his head.

I figured Nat would come over to me and tell me what he was going to do but he didn't. He never addressed the band until he announced we'd be doing the old Gospel standard, "I Saw The Light." Then he turned and gave us the key. If you were a musician and didn't know this song it would probably be your last gig. Fortunately, we all knew it and, unrehearsed, made it sound like we had been playing it together for years. It may have been the most frightening moment I ever faced at a big live concert.

Our next gig was at the Queen City Club in Dickinson, North Dakota, and he called to see if we would be able to meet him there since he was going to fly to the show. I drove down to his house and we discussed how much expense money we would need to get to the gig. We estimated an amount, and he gave me cash for food and gas money. Then I had to figure out how we were going to get there with our equipment. Jesse was the only one with a dependable car that could make a trip like that from Nashville. It was 1,400 miles and would take about 24 hours to get there. We went to U-Haul and they put a bumper mount on his car, and we attached a trailer to haul our luggage and equipment. With all the gear and the four of us in that Chevelle, the rear was nearly dragging the ground.

About halfway there, I realized we didn't have enough money to get there, even if we pooled our personal cash, which was limited. We decided we had to have gas since we would have food once we arrived, and, after all, we weren't going to starve to death in 24 hours. So, we opted for gas over food.

We were all getting really hungry and when we made a gas stop there was a grocery store in the lot next to the gas station. As everybody got back in the car, somebody said, "Drive over to that store." I said, "What?" And he repeated himself saying, "Drive over to that store." I said, "We don't have money for food," but he insisted, and I gave in thinking maybe he had some money that he was holding out on us. I'm not going to say who it was, but two people went in the store and came back with a loaf of bread and bologna inside their coats. While it wasn't my way of doing things, it sure tasted good.

Nat was one of the guys on the road. He was funny and always joking with everybody. We were staying in a band house and he was right there with us. One night Phil was laying in his bed when Nat walked by his open door in his underwear. As Nat passed, he looked in at Phil and said, "No, don't even think about it."

Little did we know that Nat would leave this world a short five years later as a result of lung cancer. He and I remained friends until his death and I continue to correspond with Nat's wife Ann Stuckey, a shrewd music industry veteran who was responsible for much of Nat's success. I learned a lot

about the music business during my time with Ann and Nat and was sad at his passing at the young age of 54. He had given a lot but we all knew he had much more to give.

CHAPTER 19: TOMMY ST. JOHN

When I got back home, I had a message from RCA saying they were ready to start a promotional tour for their new artist, Tommy St. John. They wanted the band to drive to Tommy's home in East Tennessee to rehearse and hit the road.

Tommy was a great singer in his early twenties and had those boyish good looks that made him a great candidate for a record deal. RCA Records signed him and put a great team around him that included producer Norro Wilson, who had produced George Jones, Reba McEntire, and Kenny Chesney. The RCA machine was behind him and we were excited that they chose us to back him on his promotional tour and beyond. To us, it seemed that Tommy had a real chance to become a major country star.

Add to the mix that Tommy's first single would be a song called "Stars On The Water" written by Rodney Crowell. It seemed to us the perfect way to introduce Tommy to a national radio audience.

Tommy's aunt, Joy Bell, was watching out for him since he was so young, but she supported him and his career and was there for him, and for us, if we needed anything. She had bought a nice custom van and trailer and treated us like we were all her children. In many ways, we acted that way sometimes and I know we drove her nuts skirting her rules of the road. Our time with Tommy was great and we had some amazing experiences.

Our first trip out with the van and trailer wasn't without incident. The trailer was equipped with electric brakes and somehow the brakes became engaged as we drove down the road. We began to smell a combination of burning tires and hot brakes and it brought our first outing to a grinding halt. We were delayed a few hours until a mechanic arrived and disengaged the trailer's brakes. The trailer was heavy, and it was recommended

that it have its own braking system to take some of the load off the van's brakes. The rest of that trip we had to get used to allowing extra time to get the van stopped.

One day Tommy's producer, Norro Wilson was checking the final mixes to some of Tommy's songs. Tommy invited the band to RCA's Studio A to sit in on the listening session. During that session a dark figure entered an already dark studio. It was Waylon Jennings. It was the first and only time I ever met him, but what a nice guy.

During Tommy's time at RCA, he had three single releases. The first was "Stars On The Water," which reached a disappointing #86 spot on the Billboard charts. The second release, "The Light Of My Life Has Gone Out Tonight" went to #55 and the final release, "Where'd You Stay Last Night" finished at #78. The writing was on the wall that Tommy's career at RCA would be short-lived. So many times, in the music industry, luck and timing become critical elements and neither seemed to be on Tommy's side. In my opinion, all the elements were there for him to become a big star. Still, the labels look at chart positions and sales, and, in their minds, if the numbers aren't there, they consider it a failure. For the band, being on the road with Tommy, seeing the crowd response and the talent he displayed, he was a star in our mind, and it was too bad the labels didn't see what we saw.

The biggest thing that happened for us during Tommy's career was getting the opportunity to open a number of shows for Jerry Lee Lewis. That was an unforgettable year for all of us and I will share some of those stories in the next chapter.

CHAPTER 20: JERRY LEE LEWIS

Because RCA wanted to get Tommy in front of as many new fans as possible, they arranged for us to open all the Jerry Lee Lewis shows. Jerry Lee's agent was also booking Tommy, so that was another vital link in Tommy's team. The connection was another "welcome to Nashville" moment. What was really going on was Jerry Lee was flying to all his shows on a private jet and they needed us to drive to every show and set up the drums and amps so Jerry Lee's band could use our equipment. At any rate, it was a wonderful experience, most of the time.

Many times, we would go onstage before Jerry Lee had even landed, and the agent would say, "Just play until he gets here." It happened more than one time, but one night we were playing in Alexandria, Louisiana, and we had played nearly an hour and the audience was getting restless. They didn't pay to see us doing mostly cover songs so we could sense we were losing the crowd. When I would look over at the agent, he would be waving his hand and saying, "keep going, keep going." We played 90 minutes and the crowd was getting upset that Jerry Lee hadn't graced the stage. I eased over to the edge of the stage and the agent informed me Jerry Lee was still at his home watching a baseball game that had gone into extra innings and he wouldn't leave until the game was over. I said to the agent, "So, we're done here?" and he said, "Yes." I said, "So, do you want to go let the audience know he's not coming?" And he nervously said, "No, no you do it."

Wanting to protect Tommy from the unruly crowd, we did one last song and played Tommy off. Once he was out of sight, I stepped to the mic and apologized, telling them Jerry Lee would not be performing. It's a horrible thing to be the person who has to do that. Among the boos and jeers, I stepped back to the mic and said, "You know what, we did our part." I guess the audience could hear the disappointment in my voice and real-ized we were as disappointed as they were. At that point, they actually applauded in appreciation for what we had done, and we got out alive.

A similar incident happened at a show in Joplin, Missouri, except that Jerry Lee was in the building. He came to the stage just before we went on, peeked at the crowd through the curtain and went to his dressing room. We went on as usual thinking everything was alright, but backstage Jerry Lee was complain-ing that there weren't enough people, and he wasn't going on. In the meantime, we were onstage having a big time and the show is going great. I would look over to the side of the stage from time to time hoping the agent would give me a "thumbs up" that Jerry Lee was ready to go on. The agent wasn't there and that told me something was amiss. We played 45 minutes; we played 60 minutes; and the crowd was getting antsy. They wanted Jerry Lee. They paid to see Jerry Lee and they had had enough of us and they were clapping and chanting his name.

The agent came to the stage and said, "Well, he's not going on, so wrap it up." Again, the strategy was to get Tommy off the stage, and I would handle the announcement. After all, I handled it "beautifully" the time before and I was confident I could do it again. I apologized and let them know Jerry Lee wouldn't be appearing. There were boos, jeers, mumblings and grumblings but I knew just what to say. "Hey, we did our part," I said. This was a hostile crowd. They didn't care if we did our part, they wanted their money back and I was assumed to be the person who could make that happen. I directed them to the front box office where they wreaked havoc, and we quickly got our equipment and hauled ass out of there.

I met with the agent backstage, and he told me as soon as the promoter found out Jerry Lee wasn't going on the promoter had taken the money from the show and disappeared. I asked about our pay and he said he didn't know what to do. I explained we didn't have enough money to get back to Nashville and demanded he come up with our money. He told me he didn't have that kind of money on him and so I asked for his credit card. He made the mistake of giving it to me. We were supposed to use it for food and gas, but we added a few extras on the trip home. At any rate we got our money in the end and he got a credit card bill he wasn't happy about paying.

Jerry Lee was a strange person. He was married at the time and he made his wife sit in a folding chair just off stage where he could watch her while he was performing. A couple of times as he left the stage he would be smiling and waving to the crowd and suddenly snap his head around toward us offstage and give us a "mean" look. I never understood what that meant, but he looked nuts and it was uncomfortable.

One of the many stipulations in Jerry Lee's contract was that the venue had to provide a grand piano for him to play. One night they failed to get him a piano. It was at a club in North Myrtle Beach, South Carolina, called "Cowboys" and when we walked in, there was no piano. The agent had them scrambling to find one, but it was so "last minute" that they were unable to do so. Jesse Terrell, our keyboard player, had just purchased a new Yamaha CP 70 keyboard. It was an innovative and expensive 88-key grand piano in a portable case that could be taken on the road and played night to night without daily tuning. It was Jesse's pride and joy.

The agent approached Jesse in a panic and asked if it would be OK for Jerry Lee to use his piano. Phil Fisher, our drummer, had already told Jesse that if Jerry Lee played his piano and didn't like it, he might burn it. Jerry Lee had been known to set pianos on fire in his past and that was weighing heavy on Jesse's mind and he expressed those concerns to the agent. The agent laughed and assured him Jerry Lee wouldn't hurt his piano. Jesse reluctantly agreed.

Jerry Lee came out to do a sound check and he sat down and asked why they didn't have the grand piano he stipulated in the contract. The agent explained there was a misunderstanding and hoped this piano would work. Jerry Lee messed with it a little bit and nodded his head saying he thought it would work. Since we were playing a big nightclub, I think he was OK with it. But, if we were playing a concert hall, I don't believe he would have performed.

That night at the concert, they introduced Jerry Lee and when he came out, he had a beer in his hand that he promptly sat on Jesse's piano. We were all standing on the side of the stage watching. Jesse was extremely nervous.

When Jerry Lee sat down at the piano, he looked down at the name and announced to the audience, "Yamaha huh? Ain't them the sons of bitches that bombed us in Pearl Harbor?" The crowd roared. Our drummer Phil Fisher yells out, "Burn it Jerry Lee, burn it." Jesse got right in Phil's face and threatened bodily harm if Phil said it again. We had a good laugh, but Jesse was not amused. His face was red, veins were bulging in his neck and he was sweating. This would be a long night for him.

Jerry Lee started the first song and the band joined in and bam, the sustain pedal rod came off underneath the piano. Jerry Lee stopped the song and Jesse ran on stage to fix it. Phil again shouted, "Burn it Jerry Lee, burn it." I could see Jesse, who is underneath the piano trying to fix it, glare at Phil and give him a dirty look. Once he reattached the rod to the sustain pedal, the show was on again and the piano survived. No spilled beer and no scorch marks, but I dare to think what Jesse's blood pressure was that night. If Jerry Lee had burned that piano, I feel like there would have been a homicide.

Jerry Lee had hired a young guitar player who was really good but had never played a big show. The show at "Cowboys" was his first night and he was being conservative in his playing. Jerry Lee, turned to him after the first song and said, "Son, I hired you to play guitar and if you don't start playing guitar you're fired." The kid came alive on the next song and showed his stuff. Jerry Lee was happy which meant we were all happy.

We had an outdoor concert in Florida, where there were several country stars on the show. On our way to the show, Jesse was driving the van and I was asleep in the back. Suddenly, it felt like I was on a roller coaster and I could hear weeds hitting the bottom of the van. We were off the road in the median of the interstate. As the van tilted slightly to the left, I could feel it quickly come back up the median and back onto the highway. Jesse had fallen asleep at the wheel, woke up and recovered. He immediately pulled off the road while we all caught our breath, and he relinquished the wheel.

On road trips, Jesse never seemed to have a problem sleeping. He would sleep with his mouth open and we were always trying to throw gum wrappers or candy in his mouth. I don't think we ever got one in and looking back I guess we could have choked him to death. One time, Jesse's "open mouth" sleeping habit was noticed by some fans. We were driving toward the backstage area of the show in Florida and people were walking beside the van. One guy saw Jesse and yelled, "Shut that fly trap."

We made it to the festival, and we would be opening for Jerry Lee, Hank Williams, Jr. and David Allen Coe. Hank was at the height of popularity and was the ACM 1983 "Entertainer Of The Year." Despite his popularity, he wasn't everybody's favorite and he had received a death threat prior to this concert. We never thought too much about it until they flew him in backstage on a helicopter. Before he got off the helicopter an entourage of policemen showed up, enough to create a line on both sides of him as he walked from the helicopter to a dressing trailer backstage. He came off the helicopter holding a rifle and had a pistol strapped on his side. Either he was scared of this threat or this was a major publicity stunt. He went onstage with the rifle and pistol, but he stood in front of thousands of fans and performed which made me question his motive.

There was one time we were glad Jerry Lee didn't show up. It was at an outdoor show in Pennsylvania and Jerry Lee got sick and cancelled his appearance. The agent was able to get Ricky Nelson to perform in his place, along with his Stone Canyon Band. Ricky was with Helen Blair, a beautiful girl he had been dating for three years. The only time we met Ricky was during a pre-show meal for the bands and crew. He made a quick visit to say hello to all of us. I was surprised at his quiet demeanor. He was very cordial and polite. After some typical backstage banter, he headed to the hotel and waited there until showtime. At showtime, a limo delivered Ricky and Helen to the stage and immediately swept them away after the show. It was a thrill to get to meet him and see his show, which was incredible. But we never saw him after the show other than him giving us a quick wave from the limo. Unfortunately, Ricky, Helen, four band members, and the sound engineer / road manager died in a plane crash two years later in Texas.

Jerry Lee was notorious for "rushing" or gradually speeding up the tempo of his songs. For example, he would start a song at a normal tempo but by the time he finished the song it would be super-fast. Ironically, he would often blame the drummer and bass player for the problem. He thought they should hold him back but that was impossible. To fix the problem he hired legendary musicians Bob Moore on bass and drummer Buddy Harmon. He believed all his problems would be solved since these guys played on hundreds of hit records and the band would be tight with those musicians setting the tempo. They couldn't hold Jerry Lee back either, but at the end of the night he always told them what a great job they did. They were frustrated but continued to play the gig for a while.

Tommy's contract with RCA was coming to an end, which meant we would no longer be backing him or opening shows for Jerry Lee. My future was unclear, so my interest turned toward playing on recording sessions.

CHAPTER 21: MY FIRST NASHVILLE RECORDING SESSION

During my time with Tommy St. John and Jerry Lee Lewis, I got a call to do my first Nashville recording session. I had met steel guitarist Bobbe Seymour at a club on Printer's Alley in downtown Nashville. He and I really hit it off. I ended up playing some fill in live gigs with him and he liked me and my playing. He called to see if I wanted to do a recording session he had put together for a producer from out of town and I jumped at the chance. I had learned to read the Nashville Number System charts and I felt confident, yet nervous because there were going to be top-notch session musicians there. The studio was upstairs in one of the office buildings on 16th Avenue South. I got there early because I wanted to be sure I made a good impression. We all got set up and it was time for the first song.

As the producer discussed the song with us, we all got a sense that this guy didn't know what he was doing. He had convinced a small-town singer to let him produce a record in Nashville and he was now playing the role of "producer."

We started the first song and when we got to the chorus, he stopped us and said he thought we needed to "modulate." I remember Bobbe telling him that probably wasn't a good place for the modulation, and it would make more sense to modulate after the solo and before the second verse. The producer agreed and we adjusted our charts and after the solo we modulated. I saw him in the control room waving his arms and we stopped again. He came out in the room and said, "I want you to modulate, but don't change keys." We all looked at each other trying not to laugh, since modulate means "change keys," usually up a step or half step.

Bobbe took him off to the side for a conference and figured out what he wanted was a dynamic build on the song's choruses. I always thought it was cool that Bobbe didn't call him out in front of everybody, but it was a story that has gotten a lot of laughs over the years.

I loved the creative process of recording and decided I would pursue getting more recording sessions. I found out that it was harder than it seemed since it was a close-knit group of musicians who did most of the sessions and, in the studio world, I was an outsider. I had to figure out a way to beat the system, so I started going to songwriter showcases and making friends with songwriters, encouraging them to let me produce their demos. I made them an offer they couldn't refuse just to get the experience. My cost didn't involve me making any money, but I needed the experience and that had value to me.

My first client was a songwriter from Ohio. Once she committed to doing the session with me, I had to get the musicians. I used guys on my sessions that also produced their own sessions and I would call them, and they would call me. I still use some of those musicians to this day. There are more studio stories later in this book.

CHAPTER 22: JEAN SHEPARD

T oward the end of our time with Tommy St. John, Randy, our guitar player, had gotten a job with Grand Ole Opry star, Jean Shepard. Jean had a number of hit records including "Slippin' Away," "Second Fiddle", "A Satisfied Mind" and a duet with Ferlin Husky titled "Dear John" that went #1. That song made Jean the first female in country music to sell a million records and she became a member of the Country Music Hall Of Fame in 2011.

Once Randy got the job with Jean, he somehow convinced her to let him put together a new band for her. He called me to play bass and hired drummer Kirby Bivans and steel guitarist Allyn Love to round out the band. Occasionally Catherine Styron would join us on keyboards. The band was very good and, in addition to playing for Jean, we also played a couple of Nashville nightclubs. We could cover a lot of country songs from the standards to things that were hot at the time and that made us popular with local clubs like Reel Country and the lounge at the Best Western Inn near the Opry. The clubs were kind enough to let us take time off when we had a road trip with Jean and that was unusual in itself. There was always another band or another musician waiting in the wings to take your job. There still is today.

Jean was a lot of fun, but she was also known to speak her mind and not take any crap from anybody. We all respected that, but it was rare that we saw that side of her.

At about the time we started working with Jean, the Grand Ole Opry came out with some really nice satin jackets that had a big Grand Ole Opry patch on the back. Jean purchased each one of the band members a jacket and had our names embroidered on the front. We were really proud of those jackets (I still have mine) and we were wearing them every chance we got.

One night we were driving back to Nashville from a concert in Michigan and we were in southern Indiana where we could get the signal from WSM (Nashville home radio station for the Grand Ole Opry) on the radio. That always signaled that we were getting close to home and those of us who had slept on the trip were starting to wake up. The announcer on the radio had a contest going on and was offering a prize for anyone calling in with the correct year that the Grand Ole Opry started. Randy asked aloud, "Gee, I wonder what year that was." Jean in the front passenger seat, as always, said, "Well, if you take a look at the backs of those Opry jackets you're wearing, the date is right there on it!" She was right, of course and there it was in large numbers, "1925." Good to know but not in time to win a prize - remember no cell phones then.

On another trip, we had been traveling a few days doing shows and were on our way to Virginia to play a big county fair. We were traveling in a van and we all looked and felt rough, including Jean. As we got to the town where the fair was being held, Jean told Randy to start looking for a motel so we could get a shower and rest a little before the show. There was a little roadside motel and Randy stopped and went inside to get us some rooms. He was only gone a few minutes and when he came back, he informed Jean that the motel owner said he didn't rent rooms to 'a bunch of carnies' (a reference that we were traveling with the carnival at the fair.) Jean didn't say a thing and jumped out of the van and went to the office. In a few minutes she came back out with room keys, although it took some time convincing the owner of her identity.

I was still a rock and roll fan and when ZZ Top released the song "Legs" in 1983 they did a video that featured them spinning their guitars like an airplane propellar. I decided I wanted to do that. There was a company called "Spin Strap" making the device so I bought one and attached it to my Peavey Dyna Bass guitar. I was playing the Opry and I think I'm the only musician to ever spin their guitar 360 degrees around on the Opry. I could usually get two or three full revolutions. It became quite a novelty and of course other musicians at the Opry would have me give them a private spin so they could see how it worked.

One night just before going on stage at the Opry someone challenged me to see how many spins I could do. My intent was to get at least 4 full revolutions before it lost momentum. It didn't happen. On the fourth revolution the strap failed and the guitar went to the floor. Typically, if I spun it clockwise it never failed but that night, I was spinning it in the other direction which spun it off. The guitar hit the floor and I had to scramble to get the strap back on and retune the bass. It all worked out fine but I never spun it on the Opry after that.

Another disaster happened at a show in Wisconsin. The promoter had a local band opening the show. When we took the stage to do our show, the bass player, David Woods had left his red Gibson bass on the stage on a stand. I thought it was unusual, because normally people take their guitars with them when their portion of the show was over. As we started Jean's show, I made a mental note to be extra careful not to knock that bass over.

After our show some guys from the opening band came over and we were chatting while I was tearing down my gear. All the while I'm still concerned that this bass is there and I'm being extra careful. As I got ready to leave the stage, I picked up my coat and threw it over my shoulder. The coat caught the top of that bass guitar and as I walked away, I pulled it off the stand. When I turned around it was enroute to the floor and it seemed like one of those slow-motion scenes from a movie. There was no way I could save it and when it hit the floor it went into many pieces. I've never seen a guitar shatter like that. It was then that I met the owner, David Woods. I offered to pay him for it. I offered to get him a new one. I offered to have it fixed even though I didn't think that was possible. He took all the blame and responsibility, but I never felt right leaving without giving him something. Fortunately, we have remained friends over all these years and I have been able to do some things for him in the studio at no cost that have helped relieve my conscience.

I really enjoyed my time with Jean and she actually let me sing a song on the Grand Ole Opry. We had been doing an Exile song at our club gigs, so I sang "Gimme One More Chance." It was an experience that took my nerves to a new level - but I did it and it came off great.

CHAPTER 23: HANK SNOW

When Jean was scheduled to play the Grand Ole Opry, she shared a dressing room with country legend, Hank Snow. Hank was a Canadian artist who made it big in the United States with hit songs like "Movin' On", "It Don't Hurt Anymore" and "I've Been Everywhere." He was inducted into the Country Music Hall Of Fame and enjoyed success around the world.

Hank somewhat resented the fact that he had to share a dressing room with another act, since Roy Acuff had a private dressing room. As such, Hank would often grumble when we came in with our stage clothes and instruments, so much so that Jean asked us all to drop off our stuff and get out of the dressing room until Hank went to the stage. Then we would go in, get dressed and rehearse the song we were going to do. When Hank returned, we'd all leave the room again. It was a tense atmosphere in that dressing room when we were all there at the same time, but out of respect for Hank we tried to stay out of his way.

One night it was snowing, and I left my apartment early in case the roads were icy. I lived about 10 miles from the Opry and, since the roads were clear I made it in about 20 minutes and was one of the first ones there. When I walked in the dressing room, I was surprised to see some of Jean's band were already there. I went in and hung up my clothes and about that time Hank came in the door. As usual, we all started moving out the door, but Hank said, "Any of you boys live up around Madison?" He was referring to Madison, Tennessee where I lived. I answered, "Yes sir, I live there." He said "I just bought a new Lincoln and I'm not sure how it's going to handle in this snow. Would you be willing to follow me home tonight to make sure I get there?" I responded, "Yes," and that started a favorable relationship between Hank Snow and me.

I followed him home and there were no issues, but the next time he saw me at the Opry he struck up a conversation with me that lasted 10 minutes. On future visits, he would insist I stick around and hang out with him and his band. This shocked Jean and the band, and, in fact, it shocked me. They often asked why Hank like me so much, and the truth was that act of kindness I showed him that night made a long-term impression on him.

Even though I was working for Jean several of my favorite stories happened backstage with other artists. Another incident involving Hank Snow happened when Mike Snyder introduced him on the Opry. Mike was a funny comedian and a world-class musician who played bluegrass style music. He was from Gleason, Tennessee and was about as country as you can get. Mike was one of the newer acts on the Opry and was hosting a segment of the Opry where he would introduce acts and take them off when they were done. Hank was known to be long-winded on his Opry spot and because of that the Opry would often get behind schedule. Hank had taken more than his share of time, which meant Mike didn't have time to do his final song. As Hank left the stage, Mike said to the audience, "Ladies and gentlemen that was Hank Snow." As the applause subsided, Mike said, "You know I could listen to Hank all night and for a minute there I thought I was going to have to." Hank heard him make that remark.

I was in the dressing room and when Hank came in, his face was red, and he was mad. He said, "Somebody go get Hal Durham." (Durham was the Opry manager at that time.). When Hal Durham came to the dressing room, Hank said, "I had a problem with Mike Snyder, and I don't ever want that son-of-a-bitch to ever introduce me again." Durham, who was aware of Hank's temper, got him settled down and assured him it wouldn't happen again. Durham then paid a visit to Mike Snyder, and while I wasn't there, I can only imagine how that went.

CHAPTER 24: BACKSTAGE
AT THE OPRY

There were so many funny events and "bucket list" moments that happened backstage at the Opry. I arrived early one evening and there were only a handful of people in the backstage area. I went to the Green Room area to get a drink and there, sitting by himself, was Dick Clark. I debated whether to approach him. At the time, my encounters with big stars outside the Nashville community were rare and here was someone that I had watched on TV all my life. It was a moment I didn't want to miss. I stepped up and asked if I could join him. You never know what people will say to you as you intrude on their space, so I wasn't sure what he would say. I was hoping he wouldn't ruin the image I had of him being a nice guy. Fortunately, he was very cordial, and I sat down. My first question to him was, "What brings you to Nashville?" His answer really surprised me, "I love country music," he answered. Then he laughed and explained that his production company was doing a documentary on country music legend Ernest Tubb. At the time, Tubb was still alive and would be performing later that night on the Opry.

I told him I didn't realize he was involved in projects dealing with country music. He told me he liked all kinds of music and was very much involved in this Ernest Tubb project. We spoke for about ten minutes before being interrupted by arriving artists. It was an experience that I rate right at the top of my "wow" experiences. I just wish someone had been there with a camera. But, in the early '80s, there wasn't a lot of picture taking going on, and certainly not like it is today.

Another big backstage moment was meeting actor Robert Duvall. He had just finished filming a movie about a washed-up country songwriter titled "Tender Mercies." He actually sang several of the songs in the movie. June Carter Cash brought Duvall to the Opry to sing that night. It was another beautiful experience, and he was extremely nice and enjoyable to be around. I was lucky enough to get a photo with him.

Most prominent visitors to Nashville want to go to the Opry, so I got the chance to meet a number of movie stars, sports figures, politicians and rock artists.

I am a big Dallas Cowboys fan, and I got to meet quarterbacks Danny White and Troy Aikman, and linebacker Thomas "Hollywood" Henderson. As odd as it seems, Jean Shepard was a friend of two-time heavyweight boxing champion, Earnie Shavers. He was around a lot - more than you would expect, but he loved Jean and her husband Benny Birchfield, and they loved him back. Muhammed Ali said Shavers was the hardest puncher he ever fought and though Shavers lost to Ali, it was my favorite topic to discuss when I had the chance to talk with him one on one.

I remember TV host Jerry Springer backstage a few times. Believe it or not he was in Nashville to record a country record. Needless to say, that project didn't get a lot of airplay, but it was funny to see him backstage hanging around all the country artists. I barely missed meeting President Ronald Reagan, who stopped by in 1984. No one knew he was coming, so after our Opry spot that night we were playing a club and I had to leave.

You never knew who you would see backstage and during the early '80s. A number of legendary artists were still performing. One of the people that surprised me with her demeanor was Minnie Pearl. She was constantly being asked by tourists and guests backstage to pose for photos and she was very impatient. If a tourist had a problem with their camera Minnie would say something like, "Hurry up. I don't have all night here." And her tone wasn't that she just joking around - she meant it. I have seen her walk away if the person taking the photo wasn't ready or wanted to take more than one shot. I guess it was her pet peeve.

If I got hungry between playing Opry spots, I would get a

backstage pass and go out into the audience area where we got discounts on food at the concession stand. Sometimes when you would go out front an audience member would recognize you from being onstage and would come over and talk to you. One night a young lady came over and gave me a note and asked if I would give it to Ernest Tubb when I went backstage. She said, "He knows me, and I want to see if he can get me backstage." I grabbed my food, went backstage and I immediately saw Ernest standing there. I went over and gave him the note and told him what she had said. He looked at the note and said, "Hell no, I ain't getting her backstage." He told me it was an old "friend" and he wanted nothing to do with her. I couldn't go back out front that night.

Grandpa Jones was always funny, and he and I had a few funny moments. Jimmy C. Newman's drummer at the time was a crazy man on the drums. He had an unorthodox style and played the drums with a passion and energy that was way out of the ordinary. One night I was standing beside Grandpa Jones watching him twirl the drumsticks and Grandpa said, "I wonder how that sounds on tape."

Another night, there was a female singer on stage, and she was having trouble finding her pitch. I had just bought a new turner that you could stick on your guitar and it would pick up the strings' vibrations and tell you what note you were hitting and if it was sharp or flat. Grandpa was intrigued with the tuner and asked me how it worked. Once I explained it to him, the girl onstage hit a really sour note. Grandpa asked, "How does that thing work while she's singing?"

One of the funniest Grandpa Jones stories they used to tell backstage was about Grandpa losing one of his cows. Grandpa had been on the road and when he came home, he found that one of his cows was missing. He told his friend and fellow Opry star Bill Carlisle that he couldn't find his cow and the two of them spent a day looking for it. The following weekend when Grandpa showed up at the Opry, Bill asked him if he ever found his cow. Grandpa replied, "Yes, we found her." "Where was she?"

Bill asked. "In the freezer," Grandpa said. Grandpa's wife Ramona had the cow butchered while Grandpa was on the road.

Getting back to the country artists, I always liked Mike Snyder and he was a clown backstage, equally as entertaining as he was onstage. He came by Jean Shepard's dressing room one night after he had eaten at the Cracker Barrel Restaurant. In the gift area at Cracker Barrel, they were selling a toy parrot. With this parrot you could record a phrase and when you pushed a button, the parrot would repeat the phrase. When Mike came in, he had this toy parrot sitting on his shoulder and said, "Listen to this." He pushed the button on the parrot and it squealed (in an unmistakable Mike Snyder country voice), "Porter Wagoner can't sing." He made his rounds to all the dressing rooms with his talking parrot, but he did avoid Porter's dressing room.

Mike was always messing with somebody and one night it was Grand Ole Opry announcer, Eddie Stubbs. Eddie was doing a commercial for Opryland Resort and Hotel. At the end of the commercial, Eddie directed the audience's attention back to Mike. Mike started engaging Eddie in a conversation that started with Mike asking Eddie if he could ask him a question. He said, "Eddie, I just heard you talking about the Opryland Resort and Hotel. Now I know where the Opryland Hotel is but where is the resort?" Eddie repeated, "Yes, Mike it's the Opryland Hotel and Resort." Mike again pressed Eddie, "But Eddie, where is the resort?" to which Eddie replied, "Mike, I'm just trying to do my job."

Another incident with Mike happened on a night when Trisha Yearwood performed. Mike was talking with a little boy from the audience and he asked the little boy if he liked any of the singers that had been on earlier. The little boy said, "I liked that girl." Mike asked, "Which girl?" The little boy said, "I liked that chubby girl." Mike lost it, but he couldn't let it go and asked the little boy to repeat what he said. The little boy repeated, "I really liked that chubby girl." That was one time when Mike got an unexpected answer. He received a stern warning from the Opry against engaging audience members like that in the future.

One of my favorite Mike Snyder jokes was his opinion on the subject of breath mints for dogs. He would say, "I don't know about you all, but I ain't never seen two dogs sniffing each other's breath."

There were several ongoing pranks between members of the Opry staff band. Harold Weakly, the staff drummer at the time, had placed an ad in a local "Trader" magazine where he advertised a van owned by steel guitarist Weldon Myrick. He placed the ad with a ridiculously low price and included Weldon's phone number. Weldon's phone was ringing off the hook with inquiries about his van and eventually found out who placed the ad. As with most musicians Weldon needed the phone to get work and he couldn't change the number. It was about three weeks of hell for Weldon trying to field all the phone calls and three weeks of laughter backstage for those of us who knew the prank and the culprit.

CHAPTER 25: MY MOVIE CAREER

I n 1984, I made my acting debut in a movie titled "Marie," starring Sissy Spacek, Jeff Daniels and Morgan Freeman. It was a film based on true events that happened in Tennessee in 1968. It was the story of Marie Ragghianti (Spacek), a parole board chairwoman who was ousted and blew the whistle on her bosses for selling pardons and paroles. Among the guilty was Tennessee Governor Ray Blanton.

So, you're probably asking, how did I get in this movie? I got a call from a friend who was working as an extra on the film. He told me the Casting Director for the film was trying to get his parents backstage at the Grand Ole Opry and wanted to know if I could help. As we spoke further, I simply asked, "If I get the casting director's parents backstage, do you think he might use me in the film as an extra?" He told me he'd see what he could do. In the meantime, I made arrangements for his parents to go backstage. The following day my friend called and asked me what days I could work. I gave him my schedule and I worked on the movie every day after that.

Many of the scenes were shot in downtown Nashville where the events actually happened, including the State Capitol building. As an extra most of my time was spent waiting, most days from 7 am to 7 pm or longer. Most of the scenes I'm in involve me standing in a group of people in the background acting like we were talking. One thing you would hear all day long was "don't look at the camera." I developed a trick to help me find my scenes in the movie later on. If I thought the camera was on me, I would point like I was showing someone where something was located. I never pointed at the camera, so it worked in just about every scene. They never caught on to my idea.

The Capitol building's floors were marble or granite and we had to wear rubber pullovers like rain slippers so that the sound of our walking was diminished.

Although I was in several big scenes, they never made it in the movie. Like many extras those scenes were left on the cutting room floor, a sad reality when you see the final film. However, my most prominent scene in "Marie" lasts less than 2 seconds. I can be seen in a flash opening the door for Spacek and the other stars as they enter the Governor's office for a press conference.

The one scene where I was prominent was a funeral scene where I'm playing a pallbearer. I'm seated two rows in front of Sissy Spacek and two children. I was amazed at how they could turn on and off tears. They would tell them they were going to do the scene and within a couple of minutes they could produce tears and crying — even the kids. I was amazed to see that happen in real life. Once the scene ended, they would be laughing and talking normally again.

It was another "bucket list" item and an education in how big movies are created and the amount of time and effort that goes into just one short scene. It gives me an appreciation of movies as I watch them today, imagining how long it must have taken to get an intricate scene filmed.

In 1985, I was called to be an extra in a Jerry Reed film called "What Comes Around," a story about country singer Joe Hawkins (Reed) who had issues with drugs and a crooked manager hiding his money in a Swiss bank. It's another one of those films where I pointed every time, I thought the camera was on me, and I worked on the film for two weeks. I watched the movie several time but never saw myself. That concluded my career as a film star.

CHAPTER 26: MUSICIAN'S REFERRAL SERVICE

W hen I worked with Little Jimmy Dickens, I noticed that a lot of people would call our drummer Tom Holland if they were looking for musicians. I told Tom there needed to be a service for musicians that would be available to people who were looking for musicians and he agreed. In 1985, with his encouragement, I started researching Musician's Referral Services across the United States. I found that if you signed up with an agency as a musician, they charged you a fee, and then people looking for musicians would have to call them to get your information. I came up with a unique plan.

Since the Musician's Union in Nashville didn't seem to be seeking work on behalf of club musicians, I decided it would be a good time to start a service of my own. The Union would let you post your listing on their bulletin board if you were a Union member. You had to physically go to the Union Hall to post your listing. If someone was looking for a musician, they would have to physically go to the Union Hall to see who had posted and was available. I knew there had to be a better way.

My plan was to charge a $5 fee and that would get your name on a list that I would distribute to people looking for musicians. I would mail and fax it to music stores, clubs, artists, agents, managers, venues all over the United States - and anybody else I thought might need to hire a musician.

On the list was the musician's name, instrument(s), whether they sang or did backing vocals, and a 65-character description of their choice. They could briefly list the kind of gig they were looking for and reference previous gigs they had. I didn't care what they said, but it had to be brief and to the point to fit the space available.

About a year later, I installed a hotline where a person could call in and press 1 for bass players, 2 for guitar players and so on. I was getting major artists calling me for musicians to audition for their shows and Dick McVey's Musician's Referral Service was off and running. To this day, I have people tell me that I helped them get their dream gig. We placed musicians with Alan Jackson, Reba McEntire, Tracy Lawrence and others. It was gratifying and the "Dick List," as some musicians called it, became an important Nashville tool for musicians. In its 15-year history, I estimate I placed more than 10,000 musicians in working situations.

CHAPTER 27: LEROY VAN DYKE

I had heard about artists paying a year-round salary and I found out that Leroy Van Dyke was one of them. His musicians would make a set salary every week, whether they worked or not. It allowed someone like me to create a budget and have a reliable income. I spoke with Leroy's manager Walter Bouillet, who was very professional in the way he did business. Rarely did a manager get involved in hiring musicians, but Walter was well aware of Leroy's impeccable reputation. He was certainly not going to let a musician in the band that had bad habits or intentions. I had spoken with other musicians who had talked with Walter and didn't appreciate the process. But with my background dealing with these matters in the music business, it was refreshing to see the effort. Besides that, I had nothing to hide. I was a team player and my background impressed Walter. I had to sign an agreement to abide by their set of rules, and he hired me. Leroy was known for his strict enforcement of the rules and the guys in the band were aware they needed to stay in line. As long as you played by the rules, Leroy was the nicest guy in the world.

Leroy had some big hits, including "The Auctioneer." His recording of "Walk On By" was judged by Billboard magazine as the top country song of all time. Leroy grew up near Sedalia, Missouri, on a farm and got his degree in agriculture. Ironically, he was a licensed auctioneer. Even after stardom, he continued to do auctions at fairs and livestock shows where he performed. He was well respected for his clean living and he expected that reputation to be upheld by the band.

When we did shows he would purposely try and isolate the band from the town where we were playing to insure we would be in our rooms and rested for the next day's run instead of being out on the town. That worked most of the time.

I worked with Leroy on two different occasions. This first band was made up of Don Coburn on drums, Speedy Haworth on guitar, and Colin Rozario on piano. The second incarnation of the band was Ron Guilbeau on guitar along with Jesse Terrell and Cliff Gerken on keyboards.

I can't remember where we were playing but after the show, Ron and I met a married couple that invited us to join them at a club that was a walking distance from the motel. I was not a drinker, so many times I was hanging out to take care of somebody who did. This night Ron and I walked to the club. It was a short walk but up a hill and it seemed like it took us forever to get there. The couple we met earlier were there and had a table set up for the four of us. There was a pitcher of beer on the table and they insisted I drink a beer with them. Remember, I am not a drinker. I had to turn away from the table to watch the band and every time I turned around my glass would be full. I have my suspicions that this was Ron's idea. I sipped on the beer and after a couple of hours it was time to go. As soon as I stood up, I realized I may not be able to walk. I was very wobbly, but I figured I could walk down the hill to the motel. So off we went.

As we start walking, I noticed it is a desolate area between the club and our hotel. I had to pee so I thought this would be a good spot. Ron insisted that we continue walking as I peed and that created a big problem and I peed all over the front of my pants. I wasn't too worried because we were close to the motel and my plan was to take a shower and sleep like a baby.

Across from our motel was a Waffle House, and Ron starts demanding we go eat. I said, "Ron, I can't go eat, I've pissed all over myself." As we got closer to the motel, he again said he wanted me to go eat with him. Again, I refused. Then Ron came up with a plan. He said, "There are only about ten people in there eating and they're toward the back. Let me go in first and I'll stand in front of you until we get to a booth and you slide in and we're good." Obviously, my thinking was impaired, and I agreed that his plan would work. We got in the front door and sure enough he was shielding me from the other guests. And then it happened. Just before we got to our booth he stepped out of the way and pointed at me and yelled, "Hey, look at this guy. He's pissed all over himself." Everybody had a laugh and we sat down and had a meal.

The closest I ever got to getting fired was after a show when Colin talked me into going to a club. We were in Montana and someone in the band introduced us as being in Leroy Van Dyke's band. Then came a flurry of drinks. I didn't drink, but Colin did. I never saw him so drunk. When it was time to go home someone said they were going to continue the party at their apartment. I told Colin we needed to get back to the motel, but he was getting angry, so to keep him quiet I went along. I was stone sober, so I figured I needed to take care of Colin. We got in the car with a couple and went to the apartment complex. No one could remember the apartment number so Colin and the guy driving decide they'll snoop through the apartment complex until they see or hear evidence of a party. They didn't see or hear anything that indicated a party, so Colin got belligerent and starts banging on apartment doors and waking people up. It was around 2 am.

I was waiting in the car with the guy's wife, while Colin and the guy did their reconnaissance run. I didn't realize they were banging on doors and waking everybody up, until they got back in the car and police cars surrounded us. This was a small town, so I imagine every patrol car they owned showed up. There was a lot of talking and negotiating by the driver and his wife. There was a lot of "sorry" being said by me, speaking for Colin and a lot of dropping the name Leroy Van Dyke. The police finally decided that the woman was sober and could drive us to the motel. They let us go. If they hadn't, it would have been the end for Colin and me. But this story doesn't end here.

We got to the motel and in the room and we immediately

went to bed. I could hear Colin snoring, so I assumed he was asleep, so I drifted off. At some point, I felt Colin breathing heavily near my face and it awakened me. He was squatted down beside my bed taking a dump. I started yelling at him, "What are you doing?" He jumped and said, "I was dreaming I was in the desert and I had to go to the bathroom." I screamed, "Well, you're not in the desert and you are going to clean this up." He wasn't able. I had some baby powder in my bag, so I laid a heavy coat on the pile, covered it with several towels and went back to sleep. But this story doesn't end here.

The next day on the bus Colin was extremely sick. He was throwing up, had diarrhea and made one trip after the other to the bathroom. Pooping on the bus is frowned upon, especially by those traveling with the culprit. Leroy's wife was on this trip and she kept asking me, "What's wrong with Colin?" Maintaining my code of road musician ethics, I just shrugged my shoulders like, "I don't know."

Leroy, who was driving the bus, called Colin to the front of the bus. "What's wrong with you, Colin?" he asked. Colin was tired and weak and exhausted, and he barely blurts out, "I drank some milk that must have been bad." Oddly enough, that seemed to satisfy Leroy's curiosity.

Ron was the "rebel" in the band. A great guitar player and singer but he was constantly trying to find a way to skirt the rules.

Ron had one pair of shoes that he wore. It was a pair of tennis shoes that were dirty, smelly and blown out on both sides. I don't know how they were being held together. It was apparent to us that these shoes did not belong in the confines of a bus.

Leroy hated those shoes, and he came up with a plan to eliminate them. We plotted to get Ron's shoe size and Leroy bought him a new pair of shoes similar to the nasty ones. The plan was that when Ron sat down on the bus, somebody would snatch those shoes off his feet, hand them to the next person who would douse them with lighter fluid, then Leroy would set them on fire and throw them into the parking lot. The plan worked flawlessly. But Ron was really upset that we had burned his shoes. Even the new shoes didn't seem to calm him down until later on. We all had a good laugh and it's one of Leroy's favorite road stories.

Leroy was an avid hunter and believer that "if you kill it, you need to eat it or find a use for what you killed." We were driving to a show out West, and I was in my bunk when all of a sudden, Leroy hit the brakes so hard I thought we were avoiding a wreck. He immediately came running down the aisle of the bus between the bunks and I said, "What's going on?" His only reply was "Coyote."

A few seconds later he went running to the front of the bus with his rifle. By the time I got up front he had fired a couple of shots. "Got him," he said. He and Don went running out through a field to retrieve the prize.

When Leroy got back to the bus he said, "I've never shot a coyote before," to which I replied, "What are you going to do with it?" I knew he wasn't going to eat it, so how would he make use of his kill. "I'm going to skin it for the pelt," he said. I thought he would throw it in a bin under the bus and when we got somewhere he'd skin it out. But no, he started collecting newspapers and spreading them out on the floor and skinned it right then and there as Don drove the bus. I went back to my bunk.

One time we arrived at Leroy's house to leave for a road trip. He had just killed and dressed out a deer. He took the head of the deer and put it under the bus. When we questioned him about it, he just said, "Wait and see." At our first rest stop on the trip Leroy took the deer head and placed it in the women's bathroom with the head sticking out of a toilet in a stall. We tried to wait until someone went in the women's bathroom to discover the surprise, but no one came for a few minutes, so we had to get on the road. I often wonder what happened.

We played a fair somewhere in the Midwest and when we finished with the show and packed up, the fair had locked us in the fairgrounds with a big chain across the exit gate. We drove to several gates only to find all of them locked. Leroy had been on the road so long he had a solution for nearly every problem we encountered. He had bolt cutters on the bus, and he cut through those locks like butter, and we're off to the next gig.

Leroy was very popular at fairs and farm shows because of his connection as a farmer and auctioneer. Often times before or after our show, he would auction off livestock as part of his contract. As a result, we traveled the Midwest extensively and often in areas where cattle ranching was popular.

One trip took us to Montana, and we were in a neat little town having lunch at a locally owned restaurant. All of a sudden, Leroy's wife Gladys came over to the table and said, "Dick we need you out front. Someone is having a heart attack." Having been an EMT and an EMT Instructor for the State of West Virginia, I had several occasions to put that talent to use on the road. This was the most critical experience I had. Everyone at the table jumped up and we went to the front of the restaurant where a man was in deep distress. He was slumped over in the sitting position, blue and not breathing. Don Coburn was with me and he and I picked the man up and laid him down on the sidewalk. I showed Don how to do CPR and he was going to do chest compressions while I did mouth-to-mouth resuscitation. When we laid him down, Don was nervous and started doing chest compressions immediately. As I reached under the man's neck and tilted his head back to clear his airway, Don's chest compressions had already started forcing air out of the man's mouth. As Don continued, the man started to breathe on his own and his color returned. By the time paramedics arrived his color was good, and they took over the process and got him to the hospital. I often wondered what happened to that man and prayed that he recovered.

On another occasion, there was a car accident. I was in my bunk and here came Gladys, "Dick, there's a wreck and a young boy is pinned underneath a car." I jumped up and went to the scene where a man and his son had run off the interstate and flipped their car. The boy was pinned underneath. I could hear sirens in the distance, so I knew help was on the way. There was

a nurse on the scene, and she was talking to the boy. He was alert and responsive and didn't show any signs of distress other than he couldn't free himself. It was a helpless situation other than the nurse was there to comfort him. His father was shaken but otherwise uninjured, so as paramedics and the fire department arrived, I went back to the bus. I jokingly told Gladys the next time I heard her call my name, I was going to hide.

Leroy was invited to play the Quarter Horse Congress in 1986 in San Antonio, Texas. A quarter horse is known for its speed and ability to quickly maneuver, especially when herding cattle. Every year they have a convention for owners and it's quite an event.

One of the many attendees at the convention was Carl Smith, a legendary country singer and a member of the Country Music Hall of Fame. He was known for hits like "I Overlooked An Orchid" and "Hey Joe." During the '50s thru the '70s, he scored a chart record every year for 21 years. When Carl retired from music, he spent most of his time raising quarter horses and developing real estate.

Carl and Leroy were friends and during our performance he introduced Carl and asked if he'd come up on stage. Carl came up and said a few words and planned to leave but Leroy asked if he'd like to sing. At that point the crowd response was overwhelming, and he sang, "I Overlooked An Orchid". I'm not sure, but this may have been Carl's last public performance. It was another one of those situations that gave me a rare opportunity to play bass for a legend. It was a memorable night for me.

When you travel with an artist you always have people trying to get to the artist. They'll ask you to take something to the artist or they'll want to get on the bus. It can be a tricky situation in how you handle it. We were doing a farm show in Nebraska and a man came up and asked if he could speak to

Leroy. He had the appearance of a farmer and was wearing a Ford tractor baseball cap. I asked for his name and I went on the bus to tell Leroy. I said, "Leroy there's a farmer out here who claims to know you and he said he'd like to speak to you. His name is Buddy Kalb." Leroy asked, "You don't know who that is do you?" and I replied, "No". Leroy said, "He wrote 'Mississippi Squirrel Revival' and a lot of crazy songs for Ray Stevens." Leroy brought Buddy on the bus and they had a wonderful catch-up. Oddly enough, Buddy was a salesman for Ford tractors and, even though he had success as a songwriter, he never moved to Nashville until after he retired.

Leroy was one of the most intelligent and business-minded artists I ever knew. I learned a lot from him and admired the way he handled every aspect of his career. He would set up his own sound system, work on the bus, deal with people at venues and treated any health issues in a natural way. With a degree in agriculture, his knowledge of plants and nutrition has kept him healthy and active into his 90s. He had a tackle box in the back of the bus with herbs and all-natural vitamins — nothing illegal mind you. He told me he never took a drink of alcohol in his life. He had never had a headache. He always drank a glass of tomato juice every morning. I never saw him sick. As of this writing he is still very active and still performing, a testament to his clean lifestyle and work ethic.

CHAPTER 28: THE OVERTIME BAND

I had now seen most of the United States multiple times, so I decided to find a house gig in Nashville. In the '80s it wasn't unusual to find clubs using bands six nights a week. A bass player friend named Larry Barnes was working at a club about 10 miles north of Nashville called Smeraldo's. It was a club run by two Sicilian brothers, Biagio and Giuseppe Sosta. It had a full kitchen upstairs serving authentic Italian food with the club underneath with pool tables, a stage and dance floor. Larry was tired of playing six nights a week and told me he was planning to leave. I asked him if he would put my name in the hat. He invited me to come down and sit in and I did and got the gig.

The band was called Billy Bob Shane & the Overtime Band, and the bandleader was a real Wyoming cowboy named Billy Bob Shane. The other band members were Craig Wiseman on drums (who became one of Nashville's top songwriters), Walt Houston on guitar and Rick Lisk on steel guitar. They had been working at Smeraldo's for a long time and the place was packed most nights. During the week, Monday thru Thursday we played 9 pm to 1 am, making $35 a man and Friday and Saturday we worked 9 pm to 2 am and made $50. During that time tips never played a major role in your pay like they do today, so it was rare we made any extra money.

Biagio was hot-tempered and kept a baseball bat behind the bar. He was a tough character and didn't take any crap from anybody. I often saw him beat up some big guys with that bat, as he'd be dragging them up the steps to the parking lot. Like any club there were occasional arguments, but anyone who knew Biagio knew he wouldn't tolerate one minute of physical fighting. As a result, there were very few major altercations. Biagio also carried a gun but I only saw him pull it once when a disgruntled customer decided to re-enter the bar after Biagio threw him out.

After a few months at Smeraldo's, Billy Bob got an offer to move the band to a club in Hendersonville, Tennessee, about 16 miles north of Nashville. The club was called The Eleventh Frame and, as you may have guessed, it was down a hallway connected to the bowl-

Craig Wiseman, Billy Bob Shane, Walt Houston. Dick McVey, Rick Lisk

ing alley. It was a little more money and a good clean atmosphere, so we took the gig.

The clientele was a little more upscale there and every now and then a major artist would stop by for a drink. Richard Sterban, bass singer with the Oak Ridge Boys, would stop by and have a glass of wine. Doug Phelps from the Kentucky Headhunters would come by and sit in on bass. Chris LeDoux stopped by occasionally, Skip Ewing, Wesley Orbison (Roy's son), and lots of musicians. I made a lot of friends there.

Billy Bob was a native of Gillette, Wyoming, which was home to a well-known club called Boot Hill. Billy Bob had a lot of fans in Gillette and Boot Hill asked if we could come and play for a week there. Of course, Billy Bob wanted to go home and all the guys in the band were excited to travel, so we took a week off and headed west.

A relative of Billy Bob's had a Winnebago and offered to take us to Gillette. The only issue was the Winnebago didn't have any room for our equipment, so we had to use a small utility trailer. The shows at Boot Hill went great and we had time to do some sightseeing along the way.

The trip home was a different story. As we were driving down the interstate someone looked back and noticed the trailer wasn't there. Panic ensued and we took the next exit. The first thing Billy Bob did was call the Highway Patrol to ask if we had killed anybody with the trailer and to inquire if anyone had reported the incident. There were apparently no reports of accidents or incidents, so we started backtracking looking for the trailer. Remember, there were thousands of dollars' worth of equipment in there. We envisioned the worst-case scenario, assuming it had run off the interstate and flipped destroying everything inside.

After about 40 miles of backtracking, someone spotted the trailer in a farmer's field. Sure enough, it had come off the Winnebago and made a beeline over an embankment through the farmer's fence and came to rest about 400 yards off the interstate. We made our way to the next exit and found a back-road to the farm.

As we approached the trailer, we could see the farmer standing there. We had torn down his fence so we weren't sure how he would respond. Fortunately, he was very nice. The trailer had zero damage in its miraculous attempt to escape. All the equipment was just as we had packed it. The trailer hitch had broken off but was still attached to the trailer. The farmer had a welder on his farm truck, and he welded the piece back on the trailer and we were back on the road. He refused to take any money for the fence or for fixing the hitch.

When the band moved to the new gig in Hendersonville, I started looking for a place to live there. A girl named Marsha Barrett, who used to frequent Smeraldo's, said she had a room she wanted to rent, and I took it. I loved the town and have lived in Hendersonville since that time.

Marsha worked for a company that processed credit reports and one day she came home and said they were looking for someone who could run a 90-mile courier route every day. The money was good, so I agreed to do it. Most days I would start around 11 am and be home by 3 pm, so I thought I could do that and play at night. I didn't see any reason why that wouldn't work, and I could always use the extra money. What I didn't realize was that some band members weren't happy that I took a "day job." They felt I should be dedicating all my time to the band. They started scheduling rehearsal times that conflicted with my day job and it finally got to the point that I had to move on.

As I transitioned, I started going out to clubs and sitting in with bands. I had learned most of the new country songs, so I rarely got stumped. But there was a club in Nashville called "Gabe's" a local bar and a musician's hangout, where I often got in trouble. The band leader was steel guitarist Wayne Kincaid and he was a country music purist who loved when guests would sit in and do hardcore country songs. You'd be hard pressed to find a song Wayne didn't know.

Ron Lutrick was the bass player and he and I had become friends. I walked into Gabe's one night just as the band was taking their first break. Ron came over and asked if I would fill in for him while he ran to the liquor store and I agreed, thinking he'd be back in 15 minutes. I started playing the next set and the next set and the next set. Ron never came back.

I was telling Wayne I needed to go, but he was hot-tempered and demanded I play until Ron got back or another bass player could take over. Neither happened.

That night Terry Duncan, a well-known Nashville keyboard player got up to sit in. Terry was a Ray Price fan and knew tons of Ray Price songs – the hits and the album cuts. I knew I was in trouble when he got on stage and sure enough, he called out a song I didn't know. Wayne gave me a dirty look and said something like "If you don't know that song, you shouldn't be in Nashville." He wasn't joking. Terry called out another obscure Ray Price song and I didn't know it either. Wayne was fuming mad at me. Once it was over at the end of the night, he thanked me and gave me Ron's pay. Every time I went back, we had a good laugh about it all but it wasn't funny when it happened.

It was strange but if I sat in the audience, I knew every song the band played. But when I got up to sit in, somebody would call out songs I didn't know. It was a curse it seemed.

CHAPTER 29: THE BACK ALLEY BAND

I put my own band together, The Back Alley Band, and went back to Smeraldo's and Biagio hired us. I hired Steve Sturm, an excellent singer, guitar and steel player, Greg Cole on drums, and Keith Brown on keyboards. The band was good and nice harmonies, and it wasn't long till we built the crowd up.

I remember it was a Saturday night when Daylight Savings Time started. We were playing 10 pm to 2 am. Legally, the clocks went back an hour at 2 am. So, at 2 am Biagio set the wall clock back to 1 am and demanded we play another hour. We didn't and he said he wasn't paying us. We knew his temper and didn't want to press the issue. Fortunately, he was pranking us. Whew.

One night a guy came to me after the gig and offered us a job at a club in Nashville. It was better money, even though it meant Steve and I would have to drive further. Still, it was worth it. The biggest problem was telling Biagio we would be leaving. Steve and I decided we needed to give him a two-week notice, so we decided to do that on a Saturday night at the end of the night. Biagio went ballistic, demanding we get our stuff out that night and never come back. We tried to reason with him, but to no avail. He cussed us for the next 30 minutes, the entire time it took to get everything out. We didn't expect it, since he had never shown any aggression toward us. Boy, we were relieved to get out of there without a beating.

We started playing the new gig at a club called "Chappy's" on Nolensville Road in Nashville. It was located in a strip mall and was relatively new and clean. We were drawing good crowds and the band was getting popular. Over time, as is usually the case, we changed band members. We hired a blind keyboard player named Roy McCutcheon and a young drummer named Shawn Harrison.

During the week the crowds would be moderate, but on the weekends, it was standing room only. One weeknight there was probably 30 people in the club. When we arrived, a couple was sitting at the bar drinking and about three hours into the night, they were buzzed up. They had made several trips to the parking lot. That usually meant some pot or cocaine use was going on in their car. When they finally decided to call it a night, the woman tried to take her beer with her. The waitress stopped them at the door and told the woman she couldn't take the beer out of the club. A small argument turned into a shouting match and she finally gave the waitress the beer and left.

Within two minutes the guy came back in the club waving a gun. The bandstand was located in the corner so there was nowhere for us to go or hide. The guy demanded to see the waitress who took away his girlfriend's beer, stating he would kill her. Luckily, she saw him come in and had locked herself in the bathroom. After yelling and screaming he fired a shot through the ceiling. Steve and I crouched down, Roy, who couldn't see was yelling, "What's going on?" and Shawn stood up at the drums. Shawn was wearing a banana yellow sweatsuit and was a great target. Steve told him to get down behind his drums and told Roy to get down and shut up.

At that point, the female bartender/manager on duty stepped out from behind the bar and got right in the shooter's face and told him to leave. I just knew he was going to kill her and who knows what he'd do next. I was scared and shaking in my boots. To my surprise the bartender backed him right out the door and locked it when he left. We saw them drive away, but everybody in the place was shaken. The bartender called the police, and they caught the guy at a convenience store a short distance away, buying more beer. After about 30 minutes, and after checking the hole in the ceiling to verify the gun was for real, things settled down. The bartender asked us to finish up the night, but I swear I was shaking so bad I told Steve I wasn't going to be able to play, so we went home. The bartender understood.

One downside of having Roy as a keyboard player was picking him up and driving him home every night. Because he was blind, we regularly played pranks on him. When it came time for his solos, I would often switch the sound on his keyboard from piano to some obnoxious sound. Sometimes in the middle of a song I would turn the power off to the keyboard and he would panic, but before he could get to the power switch, I would turn it back on again.

Roy and his wife were nudists and belonged to a nudist colony just south of Nashville. We played the nudist colony a couple of times and that was an experience in itself. Yes I kept my pants on.

We couldn't rehearse at the club since they opened just after noon. Steve and I lived in apartments and Shawn lived with his parents' house so the only place we could rehearse was at Roy's. The first time we went over, his wife ran around the house topless and it was really funny to watch Shawn, who was in his early 20s blush anytime she came into the room. Roy was blind, so we often questioned why he would want to be a nudist. The answers were always ambiguous, so we decided it was his wife's idea.

When we would take Roy home at night I always asked, "Why don't you have your wife come to the door naked?" He would always say she would, but she never did. That is, until one night when I wasn't there. Steve Sturm, who always protested when I would tell Roy to have her come to the door naked, was taking Roy home that night and she appeared totally nude. The next night Steve cursed me all the way to the gig.

I was always looking for opportunities for the band and I heard the Ramada Inn in Bowling Green, Kentucky, was going to hire a house band, so I called them up and asked them about the job. Since the money was better, I talked with Steve and we decided it would be a good move. There was a band playing across the street from the Ramada that was packing the place and the

Ramada wanted to see if they could match that success with a band from Nashville. Bowling Green was one hour north of Nashville and that meant two hours a day we would be driving back and forth six days a week. At that time, it didn't seem like a big issue. I offered to come up and audition for them and they agreed.

We met the bar manager and did about six songs. I could tell by their expressions they liked us, and we were going to get the gig. Roy made the move with us and we hired an incredible drummer named Chet Greenwood. The band was really good, and we started drawing standing room only crowds on the weekends. We would see the guys from the band across the street stopping in to check us out, so we knew we were getting their attention. Everybody in the band could sing and the harmony parts were a natural good fit. The bar started doing record-breaking business.

As part of our contract, we were allowed free non-alcoholic beverages, so on break we would go to the kitchen where they had soft drinks, milk and juices. I got in the habit of drinking orange juice and one night the general manager of the Ramada, Mr. Hargis, saw me with a glass of orange juice. He never said anything to me but told the bar manager to let me know I wasn't allowed to drink orange juice. The bar manager was cool with us and I explained it was a non-alcoholic drink and was covered under our agreement. She said she understood but the exception to the rule would be juice drinks. It wasn't that big of deal to me, so I respected that decision.

As spring turned into summer, the temperature inside the club would soar. It stayed incredibly hot. When we'd ask about the air conditioner, they told us it was on but couldn't keep the crowded club cool with summer temperatures in the 90s. We later found out that they kept the thermostat up in the summer to save money. With big crowds, stage lights and the heat, we would leave the place soaked with sweat.

After a few months, Roy decided to move back to his hometown in Pennsylvania, and Chet the drummer got an artist gig with Holly Dunn. We hired Dave Phalon on keyboards and Keith Kittle on drums. Dave was a mild-mannered guy. At the time, he was working as much as possible because his wife was a student at Vanderbilt University, and they were just getting by. Dave and Keith were good fits for the band. Like Steve and I, they were easy going and willing to do whatever was necessary to make the band better.

One night it was a miserably hot night in the club, and someone wanted to hear an Elvis Presley song. They didn't specify a title; so, I told Steve let's do "Blue Christmas". Steve said, "No." I said, "Come on, a Christmas song might make this place seem cooler." Steve said, "No". I turned to the audience and said, "Since they won't turn on the air conditioner, I want to do a Christmas song and see if we can cool this place down a little bit." Steve was saying over and over, "No, no, no," but I stepped to the mic and began to sing, "I'll have a blue Christmas." Dave and Keith jumped in and after about three lines Steve joined us on guitar, but I could hear him cussing under his breath. Everybody but Steve had a good laugh and we thought that was the end of it.

The following day we had an afternoon rehearsal scheduled around 2 pm. As soon as we got in the door the bar manager said Mr. Hargis wanted to see us in his office. He never called us into his office, so we started speculating and Dave started saying, "They're going to fire us. I need this job so no matter what happens please do everything you can to save this job." I said, "I don't think they're going to fire us Dave, but I promise you, if that's the case, I'll do everything I can to save the gig." My biggest concern was Steve, who was fiery and temperamental, especially when dealing with club owners. Like all of us, he had been screwed over in the past. He was over taking any crap from a corporate authority figure, who notoriously made bad decisions when it came to entertainment.

We walked into the office and, since there weren't enough chairs for all of us, we stood in front of his desk. Dave was standing beside me in a very slumped stance like he was a wilting flower. He was so nervous. Keith was a quiet guy; unless he got pushed too far, and since he was new to the band, I didn't expect him say anything. Then, there was Steve. I was very concerned because Steve was known as a "cusser" and once he started cussing there was no end. I was hoping that wasn't going to happen.

Mr. Hargis had a list of things he wanted to discuss with us most of which were very insignificant things such as me drinking orange juice. And then he asked me about my remarks about the air conditioner and singing, "Blue Christmas" in July He had been in the club when I did it so there was no denying it. I could sense Dave trembling next to me, so I apologized for making the remark and for doing the song. Mr. Hargis continued to grill me on the point and asking me why I did that. I got the feeling he was looking for any reason to beat us down. Or worse, fire us. I held my temper, talked in a calm voice and again apologized, explaining it was meant to be a joke.

Mr. Hargis said, "Well, you guys haven't been very professional here." Steve exploded and said, "You ain't either, you son-of-a-bitch." I thought Dave was going to pass out. Any chance we had of saving the gig was over at that moment. Mr. Hargis threatened to call the police because Steve had cussed him, but Steve said, "Go ahead and call the police because it ain't against the law to cuss." Mr. Hargis politely asked us to leave and get our equipment out immediately. The problem was we didn't have the van to get our stuff. So, we had to drive to Nashville and get the van and drive back to Bowling Green to load everything out. It was a sad day, but I promised Dave I would get us another job and I did. The bar manager told us later that Mr. Hargis didn't really like the idea of the club. He thought the local crowd who patronized the place actually hurt the hotel business because it was a little rowdy. When people came to check in, the noise and loud music turned people off from staying there. I really didn't think the things we did warranted getting fired, so I'm going to go with the bar manager's story.

Within a couple of weeks, I found a club in Clarksville, Tennessee, and they hired us. We played there less than two weeks when I got a call from my friend Bob Angello, asking if I would like a gig with Tom T. Hall. I told Steve I would be taking the job with Tom and I thought we should tell the club owner that I would be leaving. I introduced Steve to the owner and told him he would be taking over as bandleader. If there were any issues, Steve would be handling them.

It was my last night with the band before moving on to the Tom T. Hall gig and we had a really nice crowd. Since Clarksville is near Fort Campbell, we had a lot of soldiers bringing their dates there or looking to pick someone up. It was a fun crowd. A girl came up to the stage and asked if we knew any Elvis songs. I told her I knew "Blue Christmas" and looked over at Steve who shook his head and said, "No." She said, "Oh, do Blue Christmas, I love that song." To put it into perspective, it was still summer, but I stepped up to the mic and started, "I'll have a Blue Christmas" and the other band members joined in. Steve was mad as hell at me since it was supposedly part of the reason we got fired from the last gig.

When we finished the song, I saw the club owner walking toward the stage and chewed Steve's ass out for us doing "Blue Christmas." Steve was trying to explain that it was my fault, but the club owner said, "You're the band leader, and I don't expect that to happen again." How ironic that one innocent Christmas song could cause so much trouble within a three-week period. When we took a break, Steve was raging at me. I just said, "Fire me." And he did. Steve and I have been friends for more than 35 years now. He's one of those people that are always there when the chips are down. We've played a bunch of shows together since he fired me, but out of respect, I never did "Blue Christmas" with him ever again.

CHAPTER 30: TOM T. HALL

I n 1988 I started working with Tom T. Hall. One of the items on my "bucket list" was to play "Watermelon Wine" with Tom T. Hall and now it would become a reality. I really wanted this job. I spent hours working on the music, getting everything just like the record since that's what Tom wanted. There were signature bass lines in some of his songs that you didn't realize were there until you listened closely to the songs. They were great bass lines and very necessary to make the songs authentic. Tom wanted the bass walk up and walk downs and the signature licks to be played just like his records. He rarely would stray from that formula.

I got the gig because of my friendship with Bob Angello, a great multi-instrumentalist who also owned a couple of nice recording studios. I had worked in Bob's studios for about five years playing bass on album projects and demos and Bob and I became good friends. When he got the job with Tom, I mentioned in passing that it was on my bucket list to play with Tom.

Tom's bass player at the time was Jason Hutchison, but Jason was offered a job with Skip Ewing, a new artist that had just gotten a record deal and was starting to tour. Jason had been Tom's right hand man for a number of years, taking care of road business, playing bass and even helping Tom at his farm. When I took the job, I knew if Jason ever left Skip and wanted his old job back, Tom would probably give it back to him.

Nonetheless, I plowed forward and put together a series of charts for all of Tom's songs that indicated where the bass licks were supposed to go, and I was ready for that first gig. I rode with Bob Angello to meet the bus in Brentwood, Tennessee. I remember Bob had an SUV that had rusted through in places and I could actually see the road as we drove down. I thought it would just be my luck that my seat would fall through the floorboard and I wouldn't realize my "bucket list" dream.

My first show with Tom was in Columbus, Ohio, about six hours north of Nashville. When I got on the bus the first thing I noticed was a huge cooler. It was bigger than any cooler I had ever seen on a bus. I opened it and every inch was filled with beer. I had a six-pack of Dr. Pepper and I tried to fit it in the cooler. I was informed that the cooler was for beer and I could have one Dr. Pepper in there at a time. The rest had to go in my bunk. As I drank one, I would put another one in the cooler. These guys loved their beer. Tom stayed in his stateroom on the bus and I never saw him the entire trip.

The band members were Joe Collins on keyboards, Brian Christianson on fiddle, "Captain" Bill Swartz on drums, Jimmie Murrell on guitar and vocals, and Bob Angello on steel guitar, acoustic guitar and dobro.

A typical trip on the bus featured a lot of beer drinking and gambling. I was a little out of place but at least they knew I'd be sober enough to drive if needed. We typically drove three-hour shifts. Since there were so many of us, there were times I would only have to drive one shift on each trip. The trip to Columbus for that first show was only about six hours, so I didn't have to drive at all.

When we got to the venue, we set up and did our sound-check. Tom never came out for the soundcheck, but Jimmie Murrell had been with him so long he made sure everything would be to Tom's liking. The venue was full, and I believe that first show had 3,500 people in attendance. After being in Nashville for 6 years and working with major artists, I was used to large crowds and doing things the "Nashville way." I had become accustomed to no rehearsals with the band before a big show. I was nervous as always, but I had spent a lot of time learning the songs and I had my charts, so I was confident.

I laid my charts on the drum riser beside me where I could see them. I said to myself "This is going to be fun." As I did a last-minute check of the charts, Jimmie Murrell came over and said, "You won't need these," and grabbed my charts. I never quite figured out if Jimmie was doing that as an initiation into the band or if he meant it. Regardless, my crutch was removed from the stage. There was panic, but I was confident I knew all the songs and other than a few missed bass walk ups and downs, it came off great. I was sure no one noticed, and no one ever said anything.

A month or so later, we had a show at Carowinds, an amusement park near Charlotte, North Carolina. We had some free time after the sound check, so I had gotten off the bus to go to the park. When I returned to the bus through the backstage parking area, a woman was at the gate with a cake. She asked if I would take it on the bus for everybody and I did. Tom was there and asked me what it was, and I explained. He never said anything. A little while later, Jimmie called me to the back of the bus and explained that Tom didn't like it when we accepted food or gifts and never to bring anything like that on the bus again. I told him I didn't realize that was a problem, but I understood, and it wouldn't happen again. Jimmie added that Tom would say, "I pay you all enough that you don't need to take handouts."

Tom also didn't like it if the band ate before a show. He thought it made the band "sluggish." Ironically, Tyson Chicken sponsored Tom and we played several events for them that, of course, involved food. The Tyson people were aware of Tom's rule about not eating before the show so they would get a private room and sneak us all in for a meal without telling Tom.

A lot of Tom's songs were recorded using an upright bass. He liked that dead sound on the bass that didn't ring out after the note was hit. I experimented with muting my strings with a sponge and got it pretty close to sounding like an upright. Another thing Tom didn't like was hearing a lot of bass through the main speakers. He wouldn't allow soundmen to take my bass sound direct to the board. Instead, he wanted a microphone on the bass cabinet so he could hear the tone I was playing. He assumed that's what the audience out front would hear. We had several sound engineers put a mic on the speakers but also go direct. Tom was sharp and had a good ear. I think he caught them every time they did that. He would also ask me if I had asked them to do it. I always said, "No."

The biggest mistake I ever made in my career happened while playing with Tom. It happened at the Grand Ole Opry on national television. It was the Grand Ole Opry's birthday celebration and they had asked Tom to host the televised portion of the show. Tom wanted to kick off the show with the song "Fox On The Run," an old bluegrass standard with lots of chords with quick changes. Normally, Tom would kick off the song on the banjo, but because he was hosting, they didn't want him to be holding an instrument. The plan was that Brian Christianson would do the intro on the fiddle. We had never rehearsed it, but it seemed simple enough. I had my VHS recorder set at home to tape the show and a lot of friends and family watching on TV, so I want everything to be just right.

When you play on the Opry stage, the monitor system is often not perfect. There are so many acts coming and going that the sound crew is always scrambling trying to make sure everybody on stage can hear what they need to hear. That night they didn't have the fiddle in my monitor. I totally didn't hear the song count off or the fiddle intro, so I wasn't playing. It took me about four bars into the song to jump in. Jimmie was giving me dirty looks because I missed it, but I just didn't hear it. I was so embarrassed and then it hit me. I have this on tape, and I'll have to see this the rest of my life.

When I got home, I reluctantly rewound the tape and sat down. I'm thinking about all my family and friends that have seen me screw up on the Opry and live on TV. What am I going to do?

Fortunately, for me here's what happened. Just before the announcer introduced Tom, they were in a television commercial break. They came out of the commercial break late and my mistake never made it to the live television audience. I was spared having to see the most embarrassing moment of my life, so I never told anybody watching that it happened.

The last show I played with Tom was at Dollywood in Gatlinburg, Tennessee. It was also the last big concert at Dollywood for the year. My mother and sister had driven down from West Virginia and it was only the second time my mother ever came to see me play with a major artist.

There was a food snafu at Dollywood when we did our soundcheck. Dolly's people had brought in a lot of food backstage and when Tom saw it, he asked that it all be removed. It's the only time I ever saw a stage manager win an argument with Tom about food. He simply refused to take it away saying it was for their stage crew as well.

Dolly had set up dinner for us after soundcheck at a private dining room and we all went there to have dinner. Tom didn't argue with Dolly about the meal, which showed the respect he had for her. There was a huge crystal chandelier hanging over the dining table. As you ate dinner, the chandelier would slowly start descending down to the table. It was such a slow process that no one noticed right away. After I noticed it, I looked around and you could tell who had seen it and who hadn't. No one spoke about it until the last person had noticed. It was a funny little trick Dolly had installed to lighten up the day.

Shortly after that show, I got a call from Tom's secretary that Jason was coming back to play bass again. It was no surprise, but I was disappointed. I was ready to move on to other things. After all, I had completed a big "bucket list" item having played "Watermelon Wine" numerous times with one of the greatest singers and songwriters in country music.

Tom was one of the most intelligent people I was ever around. He was loved and respected by common folks and scholars alike. One time he had some literary professors from a major college ride the bus, gamble, and drink. I remember waking up the next morning and having to step over some of these prestigious scholars "sleeping" on the floor.

No matter the artist, I always tried to find one-on-one time with them to discuss the music business. Most of the other guys around Tom would talk about hunting or fishing, but I wanted to get in his brain and find out what he thought about things and figure out how he had become so successful.

One day I asked him, "How do you write a hit song?" He replied, "You have to write a movie in three minutes." I thought, "What a great answer." He told me his theory on writing a song was to relate to as many people as possible and "never say anything in a country song that you wouldn't say in a normal conversation." His songs are genius, and his philosophy was so simple. That's why people loved him and his songs.

CHAPTER 31: RECORDING AND PRODUCING

Around 1984, I started dabbling in recording. Having a resumé that included working with name country artists gained me respect as a musician and a trust that I knew what I was doing in the studio. I played a few recording sessions and really enjoyed the creativity and vibe of the recording studio. I was doing a lot of work with Bob Angello at Angello's Sound Studio in a Nashville subdivision called Inglewood. It wasn't the best area of town, but since Bob grew up near Chicago, he kept reassuring me there was nothing to worry about and while crimes happened all around him, the perpetrators never seemed to bother Bob. He had a street sense about him and had befriended some of the locals, so I think they looked after him and that saved him a lot of problems. And, he had a shotgun under the couch in the control room and a couple of mean dogs.

In addition to being a great engineer, Bob was also a great multi-instrumentalist. He played acoustic guitar, electric guitar, steel guitar, dobro, and mandolin and worked with Suzy Bogguss, Jo Dee Messina, Tom T. Hall and others. He had that Chicago accent and when he spoke, it was with authority and confidence. Underneath it all, Bob was a great guy and we have been friends now for many years.

I had played several sessions with some big-time musicians, so I gained confidence and knowledge that I could play and produce. I convinced an upcoming songwriter to let me produce her demos, and I hired musicians who were also producing sessions and we started working as a team. If they got a session, they called me and vice versa.

I called Bob and booked the session, purchased a 24-track

tape which was $160, a hefty price back then, and I was off and running. With Bob and the other seasoned musicians in the studio there must have been 100 years' worth of experience in the room. I knew all the guys, so my level of confidence was bolstered by the fact they weren't going to let me do or say anything stupid. The people I hired always had my back. They would make suggestions and we'd try different things until we got it right and the client was happy. Most of the time we hit the mark with our work and word spread so I got more work.

As I became more popular as a producer, the demand allowed me to increase my prices and to record in some great recording studios in Nashville. My favorite place at the time was Reflections Studio in the Berry Hill area of Nashville. The engineer there was Ronny Light and we spent hundreds of hours together doing projects. The studio owner was Gene Lawson who was well known for manufacturing studio vocal microphones aptly called "Lawson." His heart was in doing that so Ronny pretty much ran the studio and Gene would pop in occasionally from his electronics lab next door and check on things.

Recording at Reflections took me to a new level but in a sense, I still felt I was "green" to the way things were done. Here's an example. I was telling a friend of mine that I had a lot of work to do in the studio and it was going to be expensive. He recommended that I ask Ronny about a discounted "day rate." When I asked Ronny, he said he didn't think Gene would do a day rate but to feel free to ask him. I went over to Gene's office and asked him if I could get a day rate for the studio and since I was doing so much work there, he agreed and gave me a price. I asked him how many hours were included in the day rate and he jokingly said, "24." That made sense to me, but what I didn't know was that Gene was joking. A normal day rate, as I learned later, is usually 9 to 12 hours.

I set a date and Ronny and I started working at 10 am. We took a break in the afternoon and evening to eat and we continued to work. Around 10 pm, which would have been a normal 12-hour day, Ronny asked how much longer we would be working. I said, "Gene said we could work 24 hours." Ronny said, "What?" and I explained that I asked Gene how many hours were included in the day rate and he said 24.

Ronny was a mild-mannered guy. I rarely saw him upset and rather than telling me I was out of line or explain that this wasn't proper, he said nothing, and we continued to work as if this was a normal thing. He liked me and I want to believe he saw it as a challenge. We moved forward. I don't know how he sat upright that entire time, because I was on the couch, on the floor, going to the bathroom to wash my face with cold water and any other thing that would give me a second wind. Ronny remained calm and we finished every bit of the work that I set out to do. When we finished, I went home and decided to take a hot bath before lying down. I went to sleep in the bathtub.

I have apologized to Ronny many times over for my ignorance. I've bought him a lot of meals to try and make up for it. He wasn't able to work the next day, and when all was said and done, he probably ended up losing several hundred dollars.  Ronny told Gene what we'd done, and Gene thought it was funny, but to this day he has never mentioned it to me. Lesson learned.

I was fortunate enough to record an album for Loretta Lynn's daughter, Cissie titled "Rodeo Lady." Shortly after we picked out the songs and started on the project, Cissie called me and said Loretta would be coming in to sing a duet with her. That made me nervous but with Ronny at my side I thought anything was possible and I knew he would keep me out of trouble. I asked Ronny "What do I do if Loretta makes a mistake or is singing off pitch?" Ronny smiled and said simply, "Stop her and tell her she needs to do it again." Well, it happened. Loretta wasn't coming in at the right spot. I looked at Ronny but before I could say anything, she asked Ronny to stop the tape. Whew. I didn't have to say anything. Then she sang a little off pitch and again she heard it and asked to do it again. I didn't have to say anything because she kept picking up on her mistakes. I suppose all her years in recording studios had paid off, and I was sure relieved that I didn't have to correct her.

When I was able to have my own recording studio on Music Row, I had a lot of people walk in off the street looking for a record deal. I would always try to give them good counsel and tell them what to look out for in the way of scams.

Occasionally I would get a musician walk in looking for studio work and one of the most persistent guys I ever met was a guitar player named Kevin O'Donnell. Kevin would just come in and hang out and pick my brain and always hit me up for studio work. He wasn't cocky but he was confident that he was ready to play a session in Nashville. I decided I would mess with him.

We had recently recorded a song that was extremely difficult. Normally we can record a song in 30 to 45 minutes, but this song was tough, and the chart looked like chicken scratch. The song was fast and there were a lot of chords. It was hard to read and it took us close to 2 hours to record it. I told Kevin that if he could play this song in one take, I would hire him to do some sessions. He went to his car and brought in his gear. After about 7 takes, I acted very disappointed and I told him he wasn't ready for Nashville. It beat him up and he was really down. As he was packing up, I told him the truth. I still never used him on a session, but I did hire him and recommended him for many live gigs. He continues to work many gigs. We're still friends, but what a prank.

Another prank I played in the studio was on Mark Beckett. Mark is currently one Nashville's top drummers and is one of the staff drummers at the Grand Ole Opry. Even in his early days of doing sessions, I recognized his talent, and he was remarkable at playing songs right on the first take. He never had an ego or attitude - he played the songs, he played them right and you could take it to the bank that if there was a problem it probably wasn't him.

We had a session at Mike Schrimpf's SMS studio in Hendersonville, Tennessee and I wrote a special chart for Mark. The song had a stop in it, but I wrote the stop on Mark's chart in a different place than the rest of the band. In other words, the band would stop but Mark would keep playing. We did the run through and Mark was baffled that he missed the stop, so we did it again and he came out and asked me about it and I assured him the chart was right. The rest of the band knew what was going on so they started telling him he must be reading the chart wrong. He was scratching his head. Take three and the same problem. Now he's getting wise that something's not right and he comes out and demands to see my chart. He puts my chart over his and holds it up to the light. He can see the extra bar that we don't have. He threw the chart at me and called me several names that I can't repeat. He never trusted me after that when I gave him a chart. He would always double-check it with me before we played the song.

CHAPTER 32: GARTH BROOKS

I n addition to beefing up recording work, I also started a publicity company. In 1989, I opened an office on Music Row in the Buddy Lee Building, next door to CBS/Sony Records. Buddy Lee was a well-known Nashville booking agent and handled a number of major artists. His booking agency offices were on the third floor and my office was on the ground floor, right beside the elevator. Anytime an artist had a meeting with Buddy Lee or one of the agents, they would have to pass by my office to get to the elevator. If I was in the front part of my office, I could see them walk by. It wasn't unusual to get a "hello" or wave from them as they went by. If I had clients in my office, it was a big thrill for them to see a star up close.

I kept seeing a cowboy come and go regularly and it wasn't long before I found out why. One of Buddy Lee's booking agents, Joe Harris, had befriended a young Garth Brooks and signed him to the Buddy Lee roster. If I was visible from the hallway, Garth would always nod and speak as he walked by. As his popularity grew, I realized this guy was going to be a big star. Not wanting to miss an opportunity, I stopped him on his way to the elevator and asked if I could get a photo with him. He said, "I'm running late for a meeting, but we can do it when I'm on my way out." Being around artists, I knew that line was a favorite of artists to get out of doing something, so I thought he blew me off. When he was finished with his meeting, I was in the back part of my office out of sight, but he stuck his head in the door and said, "Hey pal, you still wanna do that picture?"

I went out front and he was standing there with Joe Harris, and Joe took the photo. Now here's the sad part of the story. I had a camera that used 35mm film. You would load the film in the camera and advance the film with a lever on top. Since I had only taken two or three pictures out of the 12 on the film, I put

the camera in my desk drawer until another photo opportunity came along. My wife at the time came in the office one day and took the camera without telling me. She had something she was going to do and wanted to take photos. She didn't real-
ize there was film in the camera and when she opened it to load in a new roll of film, she exposed my picture of Garth and me to the light and ruined it. I wanted to kill her. I knew there would be other opportunities, so I chalked it up and moved on.

Garth was always friendly and always took time to say hello if he passed the office and I was visible. I knew every time he hit a milestone in his career because he would send a dozen Domino's Pizzas to the Buddy Lee office staff. He was thoughtful and caring and always took time for everybody when I was around him. As he became a superstar, he never changed. If he saw me out and about at an event or at one of his press conferences, he always spoke to me and asked how I was doing.

One day I had a young boy and his father in my office discussing a recording project and Garth came down the hall. As usual he stuck his head in my office and said hello. I said, "Garth, this young man is from Oklahoma." He came right in and stuck out his hand and said, "Hi, I'm Garth," (like they wouldn't know that). He asked them where they were from and conversed with them for a few minutes. On his way out, I asked, "Garth, do you have any advice for this young man?" Garth looked around and kind of whispered, "Don't take no shit."

As his career sky-rocketed he kept me on his invitation list for celebrations, events and press conferences. His love of his fans and the media made him popular with both. If you went to one of his press conferences, he would always take time for each and every member of the press after each press conference. Several times, I got to sit one-on-one with him and asked him about how he did things from a business standpoint.

Once we discussed the quality of songs coming out of Nashville and he told me he really took a lot of time when he picked songs. He said he thought staff writers (songwriters who write every day for a publishing company) were being pressured into turning out hit songs and they were manufacturing songs, assembly-line style. The songs were written for the market and not from a personal experience and the heart of the writer. He said he thought the publishers were standing over the writers and "grabbing songs before the ink was dry" in order to get them demoed and ready to pitch to artists. "I never saw a song that couldn't get better over time," he remarked. "I think the quality of the songs would be better if they let the writers spend more time with them."

I was invited to a listening party for his album "Sevens." Garth gave a prelude to the album and would introduce each song, explaining why he thought it was important. The album's last song, "Belleau Wood," was sort of out of character for Garth and country music. We all wondered what he would say about it. He had co-written the song with Joe Henry and it's about a Christmas truce called in World War I during the Battle of Belleau Wood in France in 1917. According to the song, German soldiers and American soldiers stopped fighting and sang "Silent Night" during the cease fire and then resumed their battle afterward. I don't think the label wanted to put the song on the album, but Garth had many battles with his label over such things and usually won. When a reporter asked why the song was on the album, Garth just said, "Because I think it has a great message that we should hear and think about, and besides that - it's because I love the song."

I've seen him backstage at the Grand Ole Opry talking with people, taking photos and signing autographs long after the show was over. At Fan Fair in 1996, he showed up unannounced in the parking lot and signed autographs for 23 straight hours with no break for the bathroom or food.

I was backstage at the CMA Awards Show and standing near the red carpet, I could see limo after limo pull up to the backstage door. Every major country music star you can imagine was being dropped off. A shiny red pickup truck pulled up and Trisha Yearwood got out. Garth was driving and he parked the truck before they went inside. That's the kind of guy he was and is.

In Nashville, we heard stories within the music business of his good heart and generosity that never made the news because he didn't want to publicize everything he did.

There are a few artists who are outstanding business people and Garth is one of them. He was the nicest guy you would ever want to meet, but he was also known to be driven as a business-man. One industry insider told me, "If Garth wants something and you're in his way, you'd best move." I never saw that side of him, but I've heard some stories.

CHAPTER 33: GEORGE JONES

In the late 80s to mid-'90s, I worked with independent artists doing their publicity and promotion. A long time ago, I found out that relying on a musician's income alone was not going to give me any financial security. So, I wore many hats and enjoyed all of them.

I had a friend named Mark Carman, who was from near my hometown in West Virginia. He had come to Nashville and ran the office of Cash Box Magazine. Mark and I played music together when he was 15 years old. We played in a gospel band and he was quite a musician and singer for his age. I lost track of him until he surfaced in Nashville in the late '80s. Because I had a studio on Music Row and his office was just up the street, we visited often and one day I stopped by to say hello. The receptionist paged Mark and told him I was there, and he told her to ask me to wait until he finished a meeting. He was in the office with someone, and since I didn't have anything going on, I sat down and looked through the latest issue of Cash Box.

I was sitting just outside his office door and I overheard a conversation about George Jones. Mark was talking with Nancy Jones, George's wife. Nancy was acting as George's manager and was meeting with people learning how she could better promote George. I heard Mark say, "Well, what you need is a publicity person." Nancy said, "Where do I find a publicity person?" Mark said, "Well, there happens to be one sitting in the hall and I can introduce you to him if you want." Nancy said, "Really. Bring him in."

I spoke with Nancy for a short time there at Cash Box and invited her to my office to get me caught up on everything that was going on with George and his career. She was disappointed that the record label (CBS / Epic Records at that time) wasn't doing enough to promote George. Nancy thought George's past problems were a factor, but George had so many fans and people who loved him that it didn't make sense to me. I knew I could help her and when I laid out some of my ideas, Nancy decided to give me a shot. That day, I became George Jones' publicity person (publicist).

Everyone was aware of his drinking and drug use and that had created a nightmare for his publicity people in the past. The fact that he wouldn't show up for concerts earned him the nickname "No Show Jones." Nashville was skeptical and unsure if Nancy would be able to turn his life around.

The media seemed to always be looking for a sensationalized story, not only about George, but other artists as well. The media would run the press releases I sent out on George when we had something to say, but they were always asking about his drug use, drinking and undependable behavior. George was a smoker and would have bouts with bronchitis that would occasionally land him in the hospital. Anytime he got sick, Nancy would try and sneak him into hospitals under assumed names and even took him to an Alabama hospital once to avoid the press. Every time he went to the hospital, I could always count on the National Enquirer calling me to say, "We understand George had a drug overdose and is in the hospital." Someone close to George was feeding them information, but we never found out who it was. You had to be very careful what you said to The Enquirer because they would twist your words in a heartbeat to blow things out of proportion. I knew if that happened it would be my last day.

What I didn't realize when I accepted the job was that George wasn't interested in doing publicity. He didn't think he needed it. In his mind, he only needed to make records to maintain his status. We were living in the Garth Brooks era and country music was going through a lot of changes. George really didn't want to do the things he needed to do to keep up.

Most of my meetings with George were at his house in the living room. He'd be kicked back in his recliner watching TV and, as I discussed ideas, he would nix them one right after the other. He didn't see the value of publicity beyond what would be naturally generated by his legacy and records. In the early 90s that wasn't enough to keep him in the public eye as frequently as he needed. Because of his previous issues with the media, I think it left a bad taste in his mouth. I think he avoided anything that might put him in the public eye other than being on stage singing.

Country Music Television (CMT) was gaining popularity and I tried to discuss him doing music videos for his songs. He didn't think he needed to do it. Nancy and I had an idea to do a celebrity roast where we would bring in some of his favorite sports figures and fellow country artists. I worked extensively on the project to the point I had the Opryland Hotel willing to give us a ballroom and Jim Owens Productions agreeing to film and televise it. He didn't like the idea and didn't want to do it.

The Nashville Network (TNN) wanted him to be a guest host on "Nashville Now" when Ralph Emery wanted a break. He didn't want to do it. Project after project, time after time, he refused what I believed to be great opportunities. Jay Leno's people called and asked him to do "The Tonight Show." His response, "They don't know how to mix country music. I never sound good on those shows." It became the most frustrating time of my life. I was trying to do publicity for the top country music singer in the world and it became a losing battle.

I was so in awe of him, that I never pushed him too hard, but the one time I did, he fired me. Before I started working for him, George had agreed to participate in a radio show produced by Westwood One Radio Network, based in New York. The show was to celebrate George's 35 years in country music and would be aired nationwide on New Year's Day. Westwood One produced these shows so that deejays wouldn't have to work on holidays and instead, the engineer at the radio station would put on long play (LP) records that contained the show. As I remember, the George Jones special was six hours long and contained interviews with country stars sharing stories and giving accolades to George. Everyone involved with the project had done their part ... except George. The folks at Westwood One were on my ass to get George to do his interview. I would casually mention it to George, who would keep putting it off. It got down to a hard deadline and the New York people were yelling at me that I had to get this done. I called George and decided it was time to put my foot down. After a short discussion I finally said, "George, you have to do this interview." He said, "Son, I don't have to do anything," and hung up on me. A few minutes later I got a call from his secretary firing me. To be honest, at this point, I was kind of relieved. The frustration this job brought me wasn't worth the stress.

The next morning, I was surprised to see Nancy was calling me. She said, "Dick, George is ready to do that interview." I said, "But Nancy, he fired me yesterday." She said, "Well, I'm hiring you back. Get that interview set up and call me with the details."

It was a little confusing how Westwood One would do these interviews. The interviewer was in New York. They wanted George to go to a local radio station in Brentwood, Tennessee, where they would ask him questions that would be recorded by the radio station. Once that was done, they would send that tape with George's answers to New York and they would splice the tape, inserting George's answers.

I set it all up and went down to pick up George. I had an old Buick that a client had traded me to do a recording session. As we walked out towards my car, George wasn't impressed. He said, "Let's take my Lincoln."

On the way to the radio station, I tried to explain to him how all this was going to work, but I don't think he ever got it. It was confusing. I drove and as we talked, he was nervously picking at his jeans. I asked him if he was nervous, and he said, "I hate doing these things. They always ask me the same questions and they always want me to tell that damn lawn mower story." George was referring to the story where he rode his riding lawn mower to the liquor store.

When we arrived at the radio station and went inside. It was a blues station. "Why aren't we doing this at a country station?" he asked. I replied, "They picked the station closest to your house for your convenience." Even though I explained it to him, he thought the African American DJ was going to be interviewing him and said to me, "He won't know anything about me or country music." Once I explained that the announcer in New York would be asking the questions, he seemed more at ease and we got it done.

During the time I was working for George, his album, "One Woman Man" achieved gold record status, meaning it sold 500,000 copies. It's standard practice that when an album reaches that kind of sales that everybody on the team receives a gold record award. As things had changed over the years, there were no more gold records. The award would be a gold cassette or CD. I went to Nancy and told her I had worked all my life for a gold record and asked if there would be a way to get a gold record instead of a CD. She checked and the only gold record available for an award was George's "16 Greatest Hits" album. I asked if it would be possible to do that album instead of "One Woman Man" and she agreed.

There was an artist named Gary Adelman, who was sketching portraits of country music stars and selling them on Music Row. I had seen George's portrait there and was very impressed with his sketch of George. When I asked Gary about buying it, he told me Nancy had asked him to stop selling them because George didn't like the rendering. I asked if he would sell me one if I got Nancy's permission, and he agreed.

Nancy allowed me to buy one, and I got George to sign it and I incorporated that portrait into the award. A few months later, George and Nancy bought a new house, and on my first visit, I was surprised to see an identical Gary Adelman portrait of George hanging in the foyer of the new house. Apparently, Nancy liked it.

George enjoyed being at home and his new house had two or three ponds on the property. The day I visited, he and Nancy were showing me around the property. He told Nancy, "We've got a lot of allergy on these ponds." Nancy said, "What?" And he repeated, "We need to get the allergy off these ponds." She said, "George, do you mean algae?" and he said, "Algae - Allergy it don't matter." George was appearing that night on TNN's "Nashville Now" television show with Ralph Emery. Nancy immediately reminded him, "If Ralph asks you about these ponds tonight, please don't say 'allergy'." It was a good laugh.

A few weeks later I was at the house for a meeting with George and when we were done, he walked me to the door as he always did. As I'm walking out the door he said, "Son, why don't you get out there and find me a hit song?" I said, "What kind of song are you looking for?" He said, "I want a song that'll make fire shoot out your ass - something like 'The Race Is On'." I found and pitched several songs to him, but much like my publicity suggestions, he never liked any of them.

George loved watching sports on TV and started betting on games. My son Rob, who was 15 years old at the time, was quite knowledgeable on sports, especially football. Rob knew the teams, team members, player numbers, where they played in college and just a lot of info. I was at George's house one day and I told him about Rob and his sports knowledge. A few days later he called and asked, "What's your boy think about Cleveland this weekend?" and I would get him a report. For a while I think the only reason he kept me around was to get Rob's tips on games.

Other than sports, George's other passion was watching TV, especially "Matlock." The show starred Andy Griffith as Ben Matlock a criminal defense attorney. If George's show schedule (or anything else) conflicted with the "Matlock", something had to give. I remember being in Chattanooga for a show featuring Conway Twitty, Loretta Lynn and George. George insisted on going on first so he would be finished before "Matlock" came on.

In 1991, George left Epic Records and went to MCA Records. That resulted in the new record label "cleaning house" and replacing most of the people around George, and that included me. I had been around three years and honestly, I never felt like I did a good job for him, primarily because he wouldn't let me.

MCA Records asked well-known publicist Evelyn Shriver to come in as George's new publicist. I cooperated fully with her and actually did a few things for George after I left. Evelyn was a New Yorker and she and Nancy teamed up on George and got him doing things. Evelyn was the type that didn't cater to George and wouldn't take "no" for an answer. It was exactly what George needed in his career. He started doing interviews, he started doing videos and she revitalized him in the marketplace. Evelyn was able to do what I couldn't, and I always admired her for that.

About a year after I had been replaced as George's publicist, Nancy called me one day and asked if I could find a way to get in touch with heavyweight boxing champion George Foreman. George Jones wanted Foreman to appear in his video for the song, "I Don't Need Your Rockin' Chair". I finally tracked Foreman down at the Olympic Games in Barcelona, Spain, and he agreed to do the video. It was probably the best thing I ever got to do for George, unfortunately it was after they "let me go."

There is no doubt George Jones is one of the greatest country singers ever. I was happy to be around as he overcame drugs and alcohol and made a huge comeback, performing until his death.

His final show was on April 6, 2013 at the Knoxville, Tennessee Civic Arena. Following the concert, he told Nancy when he got on the bus that it would be his last concert. He passed away

20 days later on April 26.

CHAPTER 34: PERFORMANCE MAGAZINE

I didn't play a lot of live shows for a while after the Tom T. Hall gig. By 1991, I had won awards for "Independent Producer of the Year" and "Publicity Person of the Year."

Early in 1992, I got a call from Larry Smith, one of the Senior Directors at Performance Magazine. He asked if I would be interested in becoming their Nashville Bureau Chief and Senior Editor. I went in for the interview and Larry hired me. I wrote feature articles for them, covered major concert events and was put in a position to learn a lot about the inner workings of the music business. Performance was an international trade magazine, meaning the magazine's content was geared to the people behind-the-scenes in the concert business. They had offices in Nashville, New York, Los Angeles, London and Dallas. It amazed me the amount of clout it gave me in Nashville. If I called the president of a record label, I would get a call back, usually the same day.

I planned everything so that I would be able to do what the magazine asked me to do, but I would also ask questions about the things I wanted to know. I was getting answers from some of the most powerful people in the business, from the heads of record labels to agents with William Morris and CAA. I was also able to attend every concert and music event in Nashville and hang out with the top acts in rock and country music.

Larry was quite a character. He was the top advertising salesman at the magazine and a typical salesman, talking a lot of bullshit. He was constantly defending himself from the other salesmen, because he would encroach on their sales territories. It was so bad that one of the sales guys sent out a picture of the world with a Post-It Note stuck to it saying, "This is Larry's account."

STUDIO A

Dick McVey

Performance

As a salesman, Larry would say and do questionable things. But just when you thought he had fed you a big line about something, it would happen. He amazed me with his ability to sell. The staff at Performance started making up wild and crazy things and attributed them to Larry. For example, they made up a story that Larry was on the grassy knoll when Kennedy was assassinated.

Larry pulled off many things and he got us backstage at lots of events. I'm probably one of the few people that was allowed to watch KISS do their soundcheck without makeup. Larry got me access to take photos at a Rolling Stones concert — onstage with them. I got to meet and be around many of my heroes. He got us into the private grand opening of the Hard Rock Café in Nashville, where only 50 people were present. The musical guest was The Eagles, and I can't tell you how it feels to be standing 20 feet from Don Henley when he sings "Desperado."

Right after 9/11, Performance asked me to cover and write about the first major concert after the terrorist attack. It was Lynyrd Skynyrd and Larry got me all-day all-access. The show was in Charlotte, NC, on September 13, 2001. My job was to spend the entire day with the band and crew and report on how they felt about being the first band to perform after 9/11 and how they changed security for that show.

I was a big fan of Leon Wilkerson, the bass player, but unfortunately, he passed away in his sleep two months earlier. I was able to make friends with Leon's replacement Ean Evans, who played with the band until his death in 2009.

On this particular show the sound crew told me they were doing a kind of military camouflage theme on stage. They bought surplus Army camo netting that would hang all the way across the top of the stage. It was the kind the Army would use to cover big tanks in the field to keep them from being seen from the air. These camo covers were also meant to scramble radar and communication signals, so when the band did their first run-through, the cover wreaked havoc with their wireless mic and guitar systems. They ended up scrapping the Army cover and had one designed for them made of regular canvas. According to the crew, it was an expensive mistake.

My career with Performance got me all-day access with a lot of bands and crews. I felt extremely honored to be in the presence of some of my rock and roll heroes like Van Halen, Aerosmith, Steely Dan, Tina Turner, Steve Miller, James Taylor and on and on. I was having a blast and getting an education in the music business to boot.

My most memorable interviews for Performance were with the people behind-the-scenes in the music business. I wanted to get their take on how things got done. People like Bruce Hinton, president of MCA Records; Scott Hendricks, president of Capitol Records; Tim Dubois, president of Arista Records; Clive Davis, Arista Records and the Godfather of successful record executives; Joe Galante, President of RCA Records; Bob Montgomery, President of Columbia Records; James Stroud, President of Giant Records; and Randy Goodman, President of Lyric Street Records.

I interviewed the top booking agents in the country as well. Rick Shipp at William Morris; John Huie at Creative Artist Agency (CAA); Tony Conway at Buddy Lee Attractions; Bonnie Sugarman at Agency For The Performing Arts (APA); and Steve Dahl at the Paradigm Agency.

Performance Magazine was my dominant activity from 1991-2001, when the magazine was dissolved. The magazine owner was an older gentleman, and he was very resistant to engaging on the internet. He feared he would lose data and information that Performance had collected over the years. This data drove a lot of his sales, since Performance produced a series of popular directories geared to the touring concert industry. No matter the urging from the staff, Performance soon fell victim to not having an online presence and Pollstar came on the scene and basically wiped them off the map.

CHAPTER 35: DALE MORRIS

I n the early 1990s, I became friends with powerhouse manager Dale Morris, and we pitched a couple of acts I was working with to the labels. Morris is best known as the manager for Alabama and Kenny Chesney. He always took time to answer my questions and mentor me in how things needed to be done. He said several things that always stuck with me, "Don't ever try to make an act something they're not. If you do, they will have a short career because they will eventually get tired of playing a role instead of doing what's in their heart." It was true then and it's still true today. So many acts want to please the market, so they play "follow the leader," doing what everybody else is doing, instead of wanting to be the leader. A lot of acts never find their own voice, their own look or sound.

My cousin, Mike Lusk is a great singer, had a great look and had teamed up with a couple of fellow singers from the Opryland theme park shows (Ross Horn and John Foster) to form a trio called "Trick Rider." Like most musicians, they didn't have financial support. I found an investor, who put up the money to record three songs and Dale agreed to listen. Since his office was only a block away from my studio on Music Row, I walked over to his office and dropped the CD off with his secretary. I included a promo package with photos and a bio. To my surprise, he called me that afternoon and asked me to come over to his office. He really liked their sound and look and asked if I could bring them by for a meeting.

From a talent standpoint, these guys were the real deal and could duplicate the vocals they did in the studio live with just an acoustic guitar. That's exactly what we did. He was so impressed, he assured us he could get us a meeting with the big wigs at RCA.

RCA and Dale had a long relationship starting in the early 80s with the group Alabama. Dale and Joe Galante, the President of RCA, were great friends so all it took was a phone call to Galante to get a meeting set up. I remember going into the conference room at RCA and Dale and I sat down directly across the table from Galante. There was cordial conversation as the guys got ready to sing. I remember a total of about six label people at the table, including RCA VP, Randy Goodman and the staff from RCA's A&R Department.

The guys performed, the vocals were pristine and after three songs, Galante told them, "That's good boys," and with that, ended their audition. I was excited. I don't know how they could have been more impressive.

The people at the table buzzed with muffled conversations, when all of a sudden Dale raised his hand above his head and slammed it down on the table right in front of Galante and yelled, "Where do we sign?" It startled all of us, but Galante actually jumped backwards in his chair and started stuttering in shock. "Now, Dale you know we have to discuss this and get back to you." Dale said, "No, you don't. Let's get this on paper." Again, Joe was at a loss for words. Obviously, there weren't many people who could talk to Galante like that and get by with it. I think it totally caught him and his staff off guard.

A few days later, we got the word. Galante had recently signed the band "Lonestar" and felt they were too similar to take on another group. It was the closest I had ever come to getting an act signed to a label, so my disappointment, and that of the trio was overwhelming. So close, and yet so far.

Dale and I stayed in touch over the next few months, trying to figure out a strategy to pitch the trio to other labels without offending RCA. A couple of months went by and I got a call from Dale and he was excited. Randy Goodman, former VP at RCA had been appointed President of Lyric Street Records, a label backed by Disney. A few weeks later, after Goodman got the label set up and staff in place, he agreed to meet and listen to this "new act" Dale wanted to pitch. Dale's strategy was not to tell Randy this was a group he had listened to at RCA, but to take the chance that he wouldn't remember them.

To get the label off to a good start, Goodman had signed established RCA acts Aaron Tippin and Lari White, whose contracts were completed at RCA.

We went to the Lyric Street offices and again into a conference room. In addition to the Nashville staff there were some of the Disney executives present and Michael Jackson's agent. I was concerned Goodman would remember seeing these guys before, especially with Mike Lusk's trademark long blond hair. But he never let on if he did. Again, their performance was flawless and seemed to make an impression. A few days later we got the word that Disney didn't want to take on a new act until they were more established. They wanted to see how successful they would be with record sales for Aaron Tippin and Lari White first. There was hope the guys would still be signed, but again everything was on hold and sadly never happened.

Dale and I stayed in touch until he retired. His door was always open to me if I had ideas or questions. He's a very smart man and a manager that has had multi-year success with his acts. I wish things had been different, but it goes to show you that luck and being in the right place at the right time has a lot to do with success. It was a great experience, and I don't know how I could have asked for a better friend than Dale.

CHAPTER 36: TRACE ADKINS

I n 1994 and 1995, while still working for Performance Magazine, I got an opportunity to work with Trace Adkins, just before he got his record deal.

Trace, or Tracy as he was known back then, was working a club/beer joint called Tillie's and Lucy's in Hermitage, TN, a Nashville suburb. I wasn't his regular bass player, but always got the call when he needed someone to fill in and I worked with him quite a few times.

He liked to drink and usually about the last set, he would be buzzing from the alcohol. I never saw him where he couldn't perform, so I took a "live and let live" approach. He was doing a lot of traditional country songs, some classic rock and some of the more current country songs. It was a lot of fun and he and I hit it off.

Trace had recently had a major incident involving his second wife, Julie. She got tired of his drinking and after a heated argument decided to kill him. She actually shot him in the heart and lungs with a .38 caliber handgun (I saw a video where Julie reported it was a .25 caliber). Either way, he should have died. He didn't talk about it much, but when he did, he got emotional. I believe it was one reason he kept drinking after it happened because it played on his mind. Music was a good diversion and drinking helped him cope.

Working at Performance Magazine allowed me to meet a lot of publicity people at the record labels. The publicists were always after me to write articles for their artists. One of those persons was Rhonda Forlaw, who was the publicity director at Arista Records. One night I got a call to work with Trace and when I walked in the door at the club, I saw Rhonda sitting at a table. I walked over and asked, "What are you doing here?" She replied, "What are you doing here?" I told her I was playing bass for Trace and she told me she was dating him. What a wild coincidence.

Rhonda was a go-getter and she had convinced several labels to come and see Trace from time to time. I think Arista President Tim Dubois had actually recorded some songs for Trace but didn't think he was a good fit for the label.

That didn't deter Rhonda, and one night when she flew to Nashville from a music event, Trace was there to pick her up. It would be a lucky night since Scott Hendricks, President of Capitol Records, was also in the airport. Rhonda introduced Trace as her boyfriend and told Scott he was a singer. A few days later Rhonda asked Scott if he would consider coming to the club and giving Trace a listen. He agreed. I doubt that would ever have happened without Rhonda's involvement.

The day Scott was scheduled to visit the club, I got a call from Rhonda saying she was concerned that if Trace was drinking while Scott was there, it might botch his chances for a record deal. She asked me if I could talk to Trace and let him know how important it would be to put on his best show and leave the booze alone for the night.

I told her I would try but there was no way I could guarantee I could keep him from drinking. He was headstrong and stubborn in a lot of ways. At 6' 6" tall, Trace was a strong man who had worked the oil fields in Texas, and I didn't want him upset with me. I had been around a lot of drinkers in my life and it was my experience that you can't reason with two kinds of people —drinkers and crazy people.

I casually called Trace and asked him if he wanted to have dinner before the show. We met at the Long Horn Steak House just up the street from the club. Once we were seated, I wasn't quite sure how to approach the subject, but decided to hit it head on. I eased into it and asked him why he moved to Nashville. The answer was obvious. I then asked if his dream of getting a recording contract was still as strong as it was when he first arrived. I tried to impress on him how rare it was to have record executives actually come to a club to see an act. I also stressed the importance of this night and how much it meant to Rhonda. Rhonda was putting her reputation on the line by having Scott come to a beer joint to see him and she wanted Trace to be on his best behavior. I reminded him how much effort she had put in to making this happen. And then I hit him with the question, "So how about tonight you hold back on the drinking?" He replied, "I can't promise you I won't take a drink or two, but I won't be getting drunk if that's what you're asking. I'll give it my best." That's exactly what I wanted to hear, and I didn't want to push it any farther.

Right after dinner we headed to the club and as I pulled up to the back door of the club, the first thing I saw was Trace taking a drink. It scared me, but he reassured me it was to calm his nerves to get through the audition. When I went in the club to set up, I saw Rhonda, Scott and some other music people sitting at a table. Reality set in that Trace really was going to get a shot at being on Capitol Records.

It was showtime and we hit the stage. He sang that first set like I've never heard him sing before. It was so good that before we left the stage to take a break, Scott Hendricks was on stage and flat out said, "I'll give you a record deal." That's how it happened.

In 1996, I had a meeting with Scott Hendricks to interview him for Performance Magazine. At the end of the interview, I let him know I was playing bass for Trace that night and what a great performance I thought he gave. Scott agreed and told me he thought Trace was star material the first time he met him at the airport. He was totally convinced after seeing his performance at Tillie's and Lucy's that night. He asked if I would like to hear the songs they had recorded on Trace and, of course, I said yes. Scott and I listened to the first album, "Dreaming Out Loud," before it was released.

The label made several changes with Trace, the first changing his name from Tracy to Trace. There were too many Tracy's in the business, according to Scott, and he didn't want any confusion. They also wanted Trace to wear a black hat instead of a white one just to emphasize the difference between Trace and the other "cowboy style" singers.

Trace and I had several phone conversations after he signed with Capitol and started climbing the charts. I'll never forget the first call. I said, "How's it going?" and he replied, "Same shit, just bigger bars."

Another conversation we had he let me know he didn't enjoy some of the things they had him doing. He wasn't aware of the extra time and work it took to be a star. I asked how it was going and he said, "Well, this morning I had to get up early so I could call radio stations on the East Coast during their morning drive time shows. Then I had to have brunch with somebody I didn't know. I had lunch with someone I really don't like very much. Then I had to meet some songwriter and listen to songs. Then this evening I have to call radio stations again during the evening drive time shows. I didn't realize how much work goes into this. I thought it was hard getting a record deal, but I think it's harder trying to keep it."

Trace proposed to Rhonda during his first appearance on the Grand Ole Opry in 1996. On May 11, 1997, I was one of 500 guests invited to attend Rhonda and Trace's wedding at the Belle Meade Mansion in Nashville. It was a big-time affair, but they managed to say hello to everyone there. It's a pretty special feeling to have friends like that.

In 2013, when Trace won the NBC television show "Celebrity Apprentice," he invited Charmaine and me to a private party at the Hard Rock in Nashville. I hadn't seen him for a while and was hoping to get a chance to say hello. These events are controlled by management and publicity people and this was no exception. Fellow West Virginian Greg Baker was Trace's road manager at the time, and he was one of the first people I saw when I got there. I asked Greg if I would be able to say hello to Trace and he said, "Let's find Rhonda." He walked me over to Rhonda's table, where she gave me a big hug and immediately took me backstage where Trace was doing interviews. My friend Brian Mansfield, who was a writer for USA Today, had just finished an interview and someone else had just entered to start their interview when we arrived. The publicity person, who was trying wrap things up, was not happy, especially when Rhonda interrupted the interview to tell Trace, "There's somebody here you are going to want to see."

Trace immediately came out in the hall and gave me a hug saying, "I see the rumors of your demise have been greatly exaggerated." We spoke for a few minutes and I could tell the publicity person was getting upset we were taking so much time. I mentioned it to Trace and he said, "Don't worry about her. I'll take care of it."

To my surprise, he asked me about a song book I used to take to gigs that contained the lyrics to several hundred songs. At the Tillie's and Lucy's shows, he would always ask me to give him the song book and he would thumb through until he found a song he liked and sing it. The songs were in alphabetical order, so the first song was "Achy Breaky Heart." Every time he opened the book, he would jokingly say to me, "Why do you keep this song in here?" Trace spent a few minutes telling Brian Mansfield the story about my songbook which shocked me he would remember that and ask about it.

Trace really liked doing traditional country songs, so it was surprising when the label moved him to doing more contemporary sounding, edgy songs like "Honky Tonk Badonkadonk." When that song came out in 2005, I called him to give him some grief over doing a song like that. He said, "If you think you're mad, my Mom just called and said she was going to have to find a new church."

Trace and I remain friends and it's always good to talk to him and see him from time to time. If my friends are going to be around him, I always tell them to say hello from me. They report back to me that he tells them he thinks a lot of me. That's pretty special.

CHAPTER 37: DAVID CHURCH

I first met David and his wife Terri Church at my recording studio on Music Row in the late '90s. David has since been recognized as one of the best Hank Williams Sr. tribute artists in the country. Back then, David and Terri were trying to find their way in the music business, and I spent some time trying to help them with their careers. Terri was more of a contemporary country singer, while David was doing bluegrass style songs and traditional country. Over time we became friends and in 2000, I did the first of four albums for them.

Around 2002, David and I had a discussion about an Elvis impersonator I was working with named Travis LeDoyt. David had questions as to whether I thought he could do a Hank Williams tribute. He sang a few songs and did an excellent job of mimicking Hank. I told him he should give it a shot. He had a mullet and I told him it would have to go. He refused, so some of his first Hank tribute shows were with the mullet.

Over the years, I watched David grow and occasionally he would have me put together a Nashville band and play shows with him. There were a lot of neat shows, including one that took us to LeMans, France, via Paris in 2009.

Charmaine and I flew to Paris and had not slept for 26 hours when we landed. Terri had booked us in a three-bedroom apartment and another couple, who were friends, joined us. What Terri didn't realize was the location was near the "red light" district. By the time we arrived I just wanted to sleep. David and

Terri had already been there a couple of days, so they had adjusted to the time change and overcome the jet lag.

As soon as we got our bags in the door, David announced we had a rehearsal scheduled just down the street with the French band who would be backing him. I was shocked and dismayed that we only had one hour to get ready. I was the band leader and the only American band member. When we arrived at the rehearsal, I was a zombie. Charmaine actually went to sleep standing up in the corner, despite the loud rehearsal. The guitar player and drummer were pretty good, but the girl they hired to play fiddle had a classical background. It took a while to get her to play fiddle instead of violin.

The next day we took the train to LeMans, France, for the show. We got on board for the 125-mile trip and they said it would take less than an hour, which sounded strange. As we got underway, we were passing cars on the freeway at a high rate of speed. It turned out the train was going 200 mph.

The show in LeMans went great. They were wonderful people, but they did suffer from a lack of bathing and the odor was tough to get used to.

When we returned to Paris, we had a cab driver waiting for us with a sign that read "Duck" McVey. The rest of the trip, I was the subject of "Duck" jokes.

David had a bus, so the shows we did in the U.S. were always fun and comfortable. One time, we had a great group of musicians on board: David Russell on fiddle, Marty Chambers on steel, David Johnson on guitar, Greg Ewen on drums and me on bass. We were on our way to Minnesota to film the RFD-TV show "Midwest Country". Our driver, Sonny Barcus pulled into a truck stop to get gas. Everybody got off the bus as usual to do the bathroom thing and pick up some junk food. Sonny and I were looking at a map to see where we were going when Marty Chambers came up front and asked if he had time to make a last-minute run and grab something. We weren't paying a lot of attention, and I told him yes. We were focused on the map and as soon as we put the map away Sonny took off. We left Marty.

We were on the interstate when David Johnson got a frantic phone call from Marty. David handed me the phone and Marty told me he chased the bus for about a quarter mile as we left the parking lot. He had just missed catching up with us by a few feet. He told me he was at the Denny's in the truck stop and we turned around to get him. I handed the phone back to Dave and I heard him giving Marty instructions. "Get in a safe place with plenty of light," David said adding "Don't talk to strangers and don't worry. We'll be there shortly." Marty told me later that he was so out of shape that his attempt to catch the bus nearly killed him.

Another bus trip took us to Canada, where we stopped by Niagara Falls on the way up. On this trip, David took Greg Ewen on drums and me on bass. The rest of the band would be from Canada. Charmaine went with me, and Greg's wife Ginny also made the trip. A couple of the shows were in very rural areas and one night we spent the night in a big campground where the bathroom and bath house were a long walk away. The bus had a bathroom, but it was a big no-no to use it for number 2. It was dark when we got there and a pitch-black night.

We went to bed, but Charmaine woke me up sometime in the wee hours and said her stomach was cramping. We decided we would walk to the bathroom. Once we got outside it so dark, we were afraid we would get disoriented and not find our way back. Something had to give, so we walked to a spot we thought would be good and the deed was done. The next day as we walked off the bus, I heard someone say, "Somebody took a shit over here!" We remained silent.

One bus trip with David turned out to be my most embarrassing. We were sitting in the front lounge of the bus, where two couches faced each other. I had on shorts and one of my testicles had slipped out, dangling. David Johnson said it looked like a hearing aid at first, but then realized the real issue. Greg and Ginny were sitting across from us too and they could see it. Ginny whispered to Charmaine that "You should tell Dick to round that up and put it away." I did. I was embarrassed and we always referred to that trip as "we had a ball."

David continues to do his Hank Williams Sr. show and is featured a lot on RFD TV's "Midwest Country". Terri opens the shows for him and takes care of his merchandise, publicity and business.

CHAPTER 38: LEGENDS FEST SHOWS

My friend, agent and promoter Marty Martel had an idea to put together a series of concerts called "Legend's Fest." The show's premise was that five country music legends would tour together. They would perform their top three to four hit songs during each show, all backed by one band. Marty hired me to be the band leader and I got to work with a number of legendary artists. Among the many acts we backed were Kitty Wells, Hank Thompson, Jan Howard, Del Reeves, Freddie Hart, Jack Greene, Jeannie Seely, Stonewall Jackson, Dave Dudley, Barbara Fairchild, Jeanne Pruett, Eddy Raven, Jim Glaser, Johnny Rodriguez, Billy Joe Royal, Bobby Bare, Jan Howard, David Frizzell, Shelly West, Charlie Louvin, Pam Tillis, Leona Williams, Billy Walker, Charlie Walker, Eddy Raven, Jimmy C. Newman, Melba Montgomery, Ferlin Husky, and others.

Marty enlisted Ralph Emery to emcee the shows and the crowds were incredible, selling out shows all over the country. Since Ralph was on the shows, we thought we would work up the theme from his television show on TNN called "Nashville Now." Our first show, the plan was that Marty would introduce Ralph and we would play the "Nashville Now" theme as Ralph came on stage and welcome everybody. Ralph would then introduce David Frizzell, who would sing "If You've Got The Money Honey." The band that night was John Hughey on steel guitar on far stage right, then Penn Pennington on electric guitar, Greg Cole on drums at center stage, me on bass and Mitch Walker on keyboards to my left. Penn and John had worked up a neat intro for "If You've Got The Money Honey" and that was on their minds. The curtain goes up and Greg counted off the intro for

Ralph. Mitch, Greg and I started playing the theme from "Nashville Now," but Penn and John started playing "If You've Got The Money Honey." As Ralph walked on stage, it was a train wreck. If you've ever seen the footage of Bigfoot walking through the woods slowly turning his head, that's what Ralph looked like as he looked at the band as if to say, "What the hell are you guys doing?"

It only took Penn and John a few seconds to realize what they'd done, and we got on track. But boy was it a mess for 10 or 15 seconds. It wasn't funny then but looking back it was an experience that I can now laugh about.

On another of the "Legend's Fest" shows, the bus Marty hired had broken down and wasn't there to pick us up. It was the first chilly day of the year and we were in the parking lot in front of the Texas Troubadour Theater near Opryland. I called Marty and he got on the phone and arranged for another bus. At this point we are two hours late getting started.

We all got on board and since it was really late, everybody climbed in their bunks to get some sleep. Jeanne Pruett was on this particular show and a few minutes after everybody had settled in, I heard Jeanne screaming, "The bus is on fire, the bus is on fire." I could smell something burning and needless to say that emptied the bus quickly. Fire on a bus usually does not end well. As we piled off the bus, the driver ran to get a fire extinguisher and he came off the bus laughing. When he turned on the bus heat for the first time after a long summer, the dust that collected in the heater started to smell. After he made a complete inspection of the bus, we all climbed aboard, now three hours behind schedule, and finished the trip.

One of the craziest things that happened was during a Fan Fair show (now CMA Fest). We were playing behind several artists on the big stage at Riverfront Park in downtown Nashville. One of the acts we were backing was David Frizzell who had a big hit with Shelly West called, "You're The Reason God Made Oklahoma." On this day, Shelly wasn't there so David decided he wouldn't be doing the song. While we were onstage backing Stella Parton (Dolly's sister), David sent a note to me saying he had found a singing partner to do Shelly's part. That song is divided into two parts with the key of the song changing from David's key to a female key when Shelly sang. The note said the girl couldn't sing the song in Shelly's key, so it would be a full step down for her and then change back to David's key for the ending. I had to transmit that across the stage to all the band members as David came on stage to sing. "Oklahoma" would be the last song of his set, so between each song the band members were communicating how we were going to do the modulations up and then back down since they wouldn't be like the record.

We got everybody on the same page and David introduced the girl and we started the song. It came time for her part and the modulation to her key couldn't have been smoother. I'm thinking to myself, "This is gonna work." And it did, until we modulated back to David's key for him to finish the song. He couldn't find the pitch, but he kept singing until he found it. It wasn't pretty but he wasn't used to coming out of a different female key back to his key. I hope he learned a lesson from that.

Stonewall Jackson was notorious for giving us a song list and then changing it once he got on stage. I always wrote the charts for the songs we were going to do, so if he had stuck to his original list it would have been fine. But he didn't. I don't remember what the song was, but the steel player and I knew it and the other band members had never played it before. Once we got into the song, I signaled the chord changes to the rest of the band and we got through it. I doubt anyone in the audience noticed it even happened. It taught me a lesson. I made sure we had all of Stonewall's charts on stage in case he pulled one out of his hat again.

The Legend's Fest shows were always fun, and I heard a lot of road stories on the bus. At the time, I didn't realize how meaningful those shows would be to me. As these legendary artists pass away, I wish I had taken more advantage of the time I had with them. I believe I played on Kitty Wells' final show. Those were historic events, but at the time, I didn't realize just how much they meant.

CHAPTER 39: BILLY JOE ROYAL

During the late '90s and until his death, I got to play several shows with Billy Joe Royal. Billy Joe moved to Nashville as a part of his changeover from a rock star in the '60s and '70s to a country star in the '80s. I was always a big fan. Eddie Watson, a long-time friend of mine was his keyboard player and band leader. If their regular bass player needed time off, I would fill in for him and that happened on several occasions. He was a hero of mine from the '60s when I wore the grooves out on the records "Down In The Boondocks", "I Knew You When" and "Cherry Hill Park." It was a thrill and an honor to work behind him. His death in 2015 was a shock to all of us since he seemed to be in good health and was still singing great.

When we traveled with Billy he was always joking and told a lot of road stories that can't be revealed in this book. One thing that happened on every trip would be this exchange between Billy and Eddie. Billy would say, "How long is the show tonight?" to which Eddie would reply, "One hour." Billy would always say, "Well, I'm gonna give them a solid 45 minutes." I use that line to this day with promoters.

One night a drunk lady came up to the stage and asked for the B J. Thomas song, "Hooked On A Feelin'." Billy saw she was drunk, so he just ignored her, hoping she'd go away, or security would get her. She staggered back to her seat, but a few minutes later she came back, this time more determined. She said, "I want to hear 'Hooked On A Feelin'." Again, Billy ignored her. The third time, she came storming right up to the stage mad as hell and yelled, "Look here you son of a bitch, I wanna hear 'Hooked On A Feelin'." Billy looked down at her and said calmly, "Ma'am that's a B. J. Thomas song and I don't know it." She looked around embarrassed and simply said in a subdued voice, "OK". We never saw her after that.

One night after a show we were standing at the autograph table and a drunk guy came up, bought a CD and said, "Billy, I want you to autograph this to my girlfriend." Billy said, "I'll be happy to. What's her name?" The guy looked over at his "girlfriend" and said, "Hey honey, what's your name?" We all busted out laughing, and the guy asked us what was so funny. I don't remember what Billy told him, but I let him handle that one.

Billy Joe had been a star since he was 19 years old, so he never really had to do a lot for himself. There was always someone in his life that took care of everything for him and at these shows, Eddie was always there to take care of things. I always respected Eddie for that.

CHAPTER 40: HOLLY DUNN

In April 2002, I got a call from Steve Lohr, a drummer friend who was working with Holly Dunn. Holly's bass player's father had gotten sick and he needed to take a couple of weeks off to be with him. Steve asked me if I could fill in until he came back, and I agreed. When the bass player's father took a turn for the worse, he was not able to return and I was asked to take the job.

Simply put, Holly was a wonderful person and a great boss. She had a successful career as a recording artist, starting in 1985 when she was signed by MTM Records, owned by actress Mary Tyler Moore. In 1988, MTM Records ceased operations and Holly was signed by Warner Brothers. In 1995, her deal at Warner Brothers ended and she was picked up by River North Records. She was probably best known for her song, "Daddy's Hands," but she also had No. 1 hits with "Are You Ever Gonna Love Me" and "You Really Had Me Going." She released a total of 10 albums and had 19 chart records.

In 1997, as her recording career was winding down, she accepted a job as a co-host on radio station WWWW in Detroit, Michigan. It wasn't her first experience as a DJ, since she had been a radio host in her college years.

She started missing Nashville and many of her friends. So, in 1999, when she was offered an opportunity to move back to Music City, she wasted no time. She was hired by The Nashville Network to co-host their TV show, "Opry Backstage." A few months later, she put a band together and started touring again.

I had a series of "bus tapes," which were funny tapes you would play on bus rides to pass the time. There were a lot of parodies and funny songs and I had a recording that was a parody of a song in the movie, "Oh Brother, Where Art Thou." The original song in the movie was "Man of Constant Sorrow," but someone had recorded a version called "Man of Constipation." When I played it for Holly on the bus it put her on the floor laughing. She insisted that I make her a copy and I did. Over the two years I was with her, I bet I had to make her another three copies because she would lose them or give them to somebody.

Holly was a huge fan of the southwestern part of the United States. When Michael Martin Murphey invited her to be a guest on American Westfest near Taos, New Mexico, she jumped at the opportunity. The show was on August 31, 2002, and it was a beautiful day. During Holly's show, she had arranged a medley of her favorite female country artists and the medley contained eight songs. The arrangement was well-done, and it always got a nice ovation.

One of the songs in the medley was Lynn Anderson's "Rose Garden." We didn't know it, but Lynn was backstage and when we got to that portion of the medley, she came running on stage and grabbed a microphone to help Holly sing her song. That would have been a wonderful moment if we had planned on her being there, but it caught us all off guard. And once we finished "Rose Garden" and started into the next song, Lynn continued to sing "Rose Garden." So, we had to follow her. It wrecked the medley, but it gave me another "bucket list" moment of playing "Rose Garden" with Lynn Anderson. When I tell this story to Nashville insiders, they always ask me if Lynn had taken a drink or two. I really don't know, but all signs pointed in that direction.

The coldest date I ever played was with Holly in Flandreau, South Dakota, on New Year's Eve 2002. The high temperature for that day was 12 degrees and the wind was about 25 mph. The windchill that night felt like it was 30 degrees below zero. We stayed at the hotel in the casino, so once we got inside, we didn't have to go back outside again until we finished and started loading the bus.

The closest we could get the bus to the stage door was about 50 feet away. For me to make one trip to the bus and back took about 10-15 minutes. Two minutes to the bus and back, followed by 10 minutes to warm up and recover. It hurt to the bone. We had to make three trips back and forth to get everything loaded. I was never so happy to get on that warm bus, get in my bunk and head home.

On July 9, 2003, we played a theater in Hamilton, Ohio, and the promoter had hired a Johnny Cash impersonator as our opening act. When we pulled the bus in front of the theater, a man was there with his two grandchildren. When we opened the bus door, he stepped up and asked if Johnny was on the bus. Steve told him there was nobody on the bus named Johnny. The man looked puzzled and said he had driven three hours so his grandchildren could meet Johnny Cash and asked if we knew when Johnny would be arriving. There was a poster of the Johnny Cash impersonator on the marquee of the theater so Steve pointed out that the real Johnny Cash wouldn't be appearing and the guy on the poster was just a tribute act. Looking disappointed, he told the girls, "Well, if that's the case, I guess we'd better head home," and he left.

At the same show, the promoter paid us with cash he had stuffed in his boot. When he reached in his boot and handed the money to Holly's manager Susan Mason, it was wet where his feet had been sweating. Susan couldn't wait to get on the bus and wash her hands.

On October 25, 2003, Holly played her final road show at an annual event held in Jena, Louisiana, called "Howdy Neighbor Day." Jena was a small town with limited entertainment, so this event was much anticipated and well attended each year. It was a great event, and you could see people had brought their entire families with them.

There was a family of about 10-12 people sitting on the front row. As we were mid-song, one of the women went over to one of the other family members and punched her right in the face. One fight led to another and we had to stop the show until the police could get it all sorted out. After the show Holly said, "Well, I never thought my career would end like that, especially on 'Howdy Neighbor Day.'"

When Holly and I had the chance to talk one on one, she told me she never expected to rekindle her career as a recording artist. She did have expectations that she might be signed by a publishing company as a songwriter. Her meetings with song publishers had not been successful and that bothered her. After all her success as a songwriter it didn't seem like she was taken seriously after her record deal ended in the mid-90s. She never got their attention again. It was one thing that soured her return to Nashville, and it let me know that this was a heartless and ungrateful business. She felt like her move to Detroit had caused her to lose her status on Music Row. To add to the situation was how she was being treated by new management at the Grand Ole Opry. There were big changes at the Opry that were unpopular with a lot of the artists. One issue was management limiting their appearances. Holly had been a member of the Grand Ole Opry since 1989 and felt she wasn't being given a fair shake. She never showed her disappointment publicly, but I could sense there were a lot of things going on that were troubling her.

In April 2003, Holly came to me and told me she wanted to do a Gospel album. Her father was a minister and she made him a promise that before she retired, she would do that for him. She asked me if I would record and engineer the album in my recording studio. I was shocked, honored and flattered that she trusted me with what may have been the most important album of her career. The album was aptly titled, "Full Circle," since she started her career singing Gospel music and would be ending with an album of Gospel songs.

I went to her house on May 1, 2003 to go over the songs and get her ideas about what she wanted to do. We spent the next two weeks working long hours in the studio to make sure it came out how she envisioned it. She used the band for the album, except for me. She wanted an upright bass instead of electric bass, so I hired Dave Roe, one of the world's best upright players. At the time, the musicians in Holly's road band, "The Holiday Ramblers," were Steve Lohr on drums; Mike Sigler on steel guitar and dobro; Alan Accardi on electric guitar; Darlana Lohr on background vocals and me on bass guitar. For the album, we also used Byrd Burton on acoustic guitar, electric guitar, baritone guitar and gut string acoustic guitar; Deanie Richardson on fiddle and mandolin; Rod Fletcher and Susan Mason on background vocals. In addition to singing lead and background vocals, Holly also contributed by playing a penny whistle and autoharp. She had written four of the songs, one especially for her Dad. In the liner notes she wrote something that touches me to this day, "Dick, this project would not have been possible without your invaluable help and good ears. Thank you from the bottom of my heart."

On October 10, 2003, Holly called us all together and apologetically announced she was ending her singing career and moving to New Mexico to pursue her passion for art. It was unexpected, but I think we all knew she had had enough. We all understood the reasons and respected her decision. We saw things happen that shouldn't have happened to her and things done that couldn't be undone. It was one of my saddest times, and I knew it hurt her deeply to make that decision.

I think the final blow that pushed her into retirement came when the Opry denied her a spot on the televised portion of the Grand Ole Opry to sing the song she had written especially for her Dad titled, "I Know It's Heaven Where You Are." That seemed to hurt her a lot.

My last show with Holly was on November 1, 2003, at the Grand Ole Opry's original home, the Ryman Auditorium. The Opry would move to the Ryman during the winter months and back to the newer Opry house in the Spring. I realized this would probably be my last time to play the Opry, so I cherished every moment.

I was sad for Holly and our band family, but I was also feeling sad for myself. It was unlike me to get emotional, but I felt like this would be the end of me playing the Opry. I had performed on that stage off and on for more than 20 years so saying goodbye to those times and memories was difficult.

Every time I played the Opry, I would always flashback and

reflect on my life in West Virginia and how far music had taken me. That night was even more special. I had flashbacks to my entire life as a musician and how far I'd come. My thoughts went back to practicing by myself in the bedroom until my fingers bled. Practicing with the band in the attic and on that front porch in Amigo, West Virginia. I recalled listening to the Grand Ole Opry on the radio. Back then it felt like it was a million miles away and that I'd probably never see it in person. I wish my Dad had lived long enough to see me play there. All these thoughts followed me as we got the call to come to the stage. When I got on stage I looked around and thought what a life I've lived. I wish I had relished these moments more in the past. I looked over at Holly and blew her a kiss. We all knew this was it. It was the last time we would play behind Holly and the last time most of us would play the Opry.

That night hurt in more ways than one. But it made me want to encourage and help people who may have been dreaming and felt their dreams were unreachable. I was living proof that you can do this if you want it bad enough and work hard to make it happen.

So, Holly went off to a new adventure and we all hoped it would be fulfilling for her. Her mother was a painter and Holly had followed in her footsteps. Holly remarked in an interview once that, "the only reason I do music is to pay for my art supplies." She really enjoyed Southwestern art and one of her goals was to move to New Mexico and open her own art gallery. She called me one day excited to tell me that Paul McCartney had visited her gallery. She was over the moon. She seemed very happy once she was there.

We talked on the phone occasionally before her death in 2016. We shared the same sense of humor and I could always make her laugh. I never knew how serious her illness had gotten and even that last phone call she seemed to be her always-bubbly self.

CHAPTER 41: TRAVIS LEDOYT

PHOTO BY MICHAEL GOMEZ

I n 2000, I was hired to do promotion and publicity for a Rockabilly Festival that was going to take place in Jackson, Tennessee, the hometown of Carl Perkins. There was quite a bit of interest in the festival and many of the rockabilly and country artists wanted to help make it a success. As a result, a lot of them gave their time to perform. It became sort of a homecoming event for many of them who hadn't seen each other for a number of years and because Carl was still alive at the time, a lot of them wanted to see and perform with him.

Henry Harrison, a Jackson businessman who grew up with Elvis in Memphis, started the festival. He was a friend of Carl Perkins and had a genuine love of the music of the 50s. He founded the Rockabilly Hall Of Fame International and established a museum in downtown Jackson.

Henry and I had our disagreements about how things needed to be done, and he was constantly changing things that we agreed to do. It created a lot of confusion and caused me a lot of grief. One thing I learned was that no matter what he did, I could find a way to fix it, so as he would set fires, I would put them out. Henry was a good person and he meant well, and I worked on the festival with him for three years.

We had a lot of great artists and legends coming to the festival, and that put me in a position where I was once again able to ask a lot of questions about the music business. I did a series of interviews on film that are still somewhere in Jackson. Since Henry's death another person has taken over the museum and uncovered a lot of the work I did. Among the treasure of interviews are chats with The Jordanaires; D. J. Fontana (Elvis Presley's drummer); famed recording engineer and singer Cowboy Jack Clement; Maria Elena, the widow of Buddy Holly; Tommy Allsup, guitar player for Buddy Holly; Bill Haley's Original Comets; Wanda Jackson; Brenda Lee and on and on.

It was at the Rockabilly Festival in 2000 that I first met Travis LeDoyt. I was standing in front of the main stage talking with D. J. Fontana. There was no one else in the stage area at that time and right in the middle of talking with D. J., he stopped me and said, "I want you to look at that." I looked up and walking across the parking lot was Travis LeDoyt. D. J. was amazed at how much Travis looked like young Elvis, and that surprised me since D. J. was Elvis's first drummer and knew him well as a young man.

Later that night, Travis performed on the festival with Marty Stuart, Stan Perkins (Carl's son) on guitar and D. J. playing drums. When D. J. came off stage, the first thing he said to me was, "That's as close as you'll get to seeing Elvis in the 50s." I would later get his permission to use that phrase in Travis's promotional materials.

I really liked Travis both as an entertainer and as a person. He was nice, he was humble, and I realized his big heart may get him into trouble with the sharks that swim around in the music business. I knew there would be people grabbing at him from many directions to get him to sign agreements to do this and

APPALACHIAN DREAMER

that. I approached him and told him before he signed anything, I would like to have a talk with him. We had a brief meeting and I told him I would be glad to advise him. After the meeting he went on his way, but we remained in touch.

As we continued to communicate and get to know each other he asked if he could come to Nashville and have a meeting with me. He wanted to discuss a situation where he had been recruited to be part of an album of rockabilly artists and was told they were going to record a five songs with him and choose two to put on an album with other rockabilly artists as part of a compilation album. One thing about Travis, if he told you he was going to do something he would stand by his word. In the end, Travis recorded five songs and they used them all on the album. He was never paid for his work. I think that sent up an alarm for him and I remarked that would never have happened if I had been his manager.

I had warned him that people would use and abuse him, and I asked him to allow me to handle his career and keep him out of trouble. We had had a few meetings and I think he sensed I was someone he could trust and wasn't just "about the money." We signed a one-year agreement and I told him that if he wasn't happy after the first year, we would go our separate ways. We have been together ever since and never had another written agreement after that.

Back then, Travis was doing Elvis songs from the 50s and a lot of those early rockabilly style songs required an upright bass guitar. During that time Travis and I both felt we needed to maintain the authenticity of the show, which meant I wouldn't be playing bass. We decided we would hire an authentic three-piece band like Elvis used back then in the mid 50s. It was raw, it was authentic, and audiences ate it up, especially the ladies.

I had heard The New York Times was looking for an Elvis-lookalike to be featured in a photo shoot that was to take place at Sam Phillip's Studio in Memphis. Once I got the go-ahead from Travis, I submitted photos we had taken in Nashville and once they saw his photos, they declared him "the person who looked most like young Elvis." Travis was featured in an article in the Sunday edition of the newspaper on May 27, 2001 that reached nearly 2 million households.

I hired agent and longtime friend Marty Martel to book Travis. Right off the bat, he got us a gig at Casino Magic in Bay St. Louis, Mississippi. We started there on April 2, 2001. David Hilbert was the entertainment director at the casino. David had them build a stage as you entered the front door of the casino. There was a bar behind the audience, so it was a convenient moneymaker for the casino. Travis performed nightly there for one week. The shows went incredibly well and for Travis this was a dream come true. Just a couple of months earlier, he was working as a projectionist at a movie theater making $6 an hour in his hometown of Greenfield, Massachusetts.

Travis's ability to mimic Elvis's voice, his natural sense of humor and wit on stage, and his playful interaction with the audience started a love affair with both entertainment buyers and fans.

That first series of shows also gave Travis a lesson in learning how things you say on stage can be misinterpreted and get you called into the office. During one show Travis made a joke about the maids in the hotel might be taking things and one of the maids was in the audience and mentioned it to her supervisor. The next day we were called into the office and Travis was admonished for the remark. No matter how much we argued it was just a joke, Travis had to apologize to the maids, and he went a step further by buying them flowers. Sometimes corporate executives do not have a sense of humor especially in this era of political correctness.

At the end of that first week, the casino gave Travis a check and cashed it for him. It was quite a bit of money and when we got to his room, he threw the cash on the bed and rolled around in it for a while. It was so much fun watching him enjoying this moment and being his lighthearted self. The next day he told me he wanted to buy a new computer and he went to the store and paid cash for it. He was never able to do anything like that before.

Based on the response he received during that first week, we were both elated that we were doing something that was going to be successful. We continued to play Casino Magic every few months until Hurricane Katrina caused extensive damage on August 29, 2005 and they closed.

We continued to have successful shows until 9/11 happened. It slowed things down for a lot of people, but especially new acts like Travis trying to get started. Venues were reevaluating their security procedures and they were not booking a lot of shows during that process.

We were working at every opportunity including taking dates at places where a lot of acts wouldn't go because of their locations and bad weather. We worked during the winter in Minnesota, Iowa, Michigan and Wisconsin and Indian casinos throughout the Midwest and the south. I think that's why we are still popular in many of those areas and continue to work there. As 9/11 faded into history we started a run that we continue today and have worked around the world.

In the summer of 2002, I got a call from an agent in Las Vegas asking if Travis was available to do a big show on August 23, 2002 in Santiago, Chile. The event would include events with D. J. Fontana, Elvis's drummer in the 50s and Joe Esposito, Elvis's road manager. The show would feature a full band and would be televised live to over 5 million viewers and a live audience of more than 4,000. There was no budget for me to go, but I knew it would be a huge boost for Travis's career for him to be involved. I'm sure D. J. Fontana had a lot to do with Travis getting the call.

The agent in Las Vegas had that New Yorker "crime boss" voice and that got my attention. Usually, people like that are the real deal and typically don't wait around too long for an answer before calling someone else. Since D. J. and Joe were on the bill, I felt the show was legit and I was comfortable they would keep an eye on Travis, and all would be well.

So, Travis did the show and when he got back to Nashville, he told me he was going to visit his father for a few days in

Massachusetts. I never thought much about it until I got a call from the agent in Las Vegas. He was short and to the point, "Hey McVey, what's your kid doing back in Chile?" I assured him Travis was in Massachusetts, but he came back and said, "Your kid is in Chile playing shows with a local band. I don't like it and I want him out of there. I spent a lot of money to get him down there and now he's gone back and playing shows. You've got two days to get him home."

I immediately got on the phone and called Travis's dad Chuck, and when I asked for Travis, he covered for him saying he wasn't around. "I said Chuck, I know he's back in Chile and the promoter is very upset. He's given me two days to get him home." That got Chuck's attention and he gave me a number to reach Travis. When I called, Travis thought I was kidding and sort of laughed it off, but I told him we were dealing with some serious people and if he didn't come home it might not end well. The contract with the Las Vegas agent prohibited Travis from playing again in Chile for a certain amount of time so I feared there might be a lawsuit for breach of contract or worse. Travis promised me he would come home the next day. I called the agent to let him know, and I could tell he was upset with me since he thought I had lied to him the day before.

The next day I got a call from Travis saying he's is in the hospital and won't be able to catch his flight. He has contracted Hepatitis via what he believed was eating soup made with local water. He was really sick and the doctors wanted to keep him in the hospital one or two days.

Wow, now I have to call this guy in Vegas and try to explain this one. To my surprise, when I called, the agent in Vegas already knew Travis was in the hospital. He obviously had a good network of information on the ground in Chile, which made the scenario scarier for me. He said, "When he gets out of the hospital, I want him on the next plane home." I agreed and it happened.

After a lot of explaining, Travis admitted he got caught up with a band he met in Chile and they asked him to come back and do some shows with them. He was green and didn't know any better, but I explained to him that it's a big no-no with promoters and agents.

About three months later we did a private birthday party for the wife of a wealthy man in Andalusia, Alabama. They owned a beautiful horse farm, and the stage was set up in an immaculate show arena where they normally showed horses. This was our first show after Travis returned from Chile and I noticed he still had a yellow tint to his skin from the Hepatitis. I don't think anybody else would have noticed but I could see it wasn't his normal skin tone.

The next morning when we went over to do the sound check Travis was sick. He was lethargic and weak and looked horrible. I took him to the Emergency Room where a doctor checked him out and said he was having a relapse reaction to the Hepatitis. I told the doctor we had a show that night and asked what he thought. The doctor said it was an unusual case because Travis did not have a fever associated with his symptoms. He asked Travis if he felt like he could perform, and Travis said he thought he could. The doctor stated that if he started running a fever he would advise him not to perform, but otherwise he signed off that Travis could do the show.

They brought an RV to the back door of the arena so after we got dressed for the show at the hotel, we went to the RV. Travis was in horrible shape. The worst I had ever seen any entertainer about to do a show.

The band went on stage and when I introduced him, he hit the stage running. You would never know it was the same person I had been with five minutes before. He sang, he danced, he went into the crowd, and he did a show like any other. I was amazed, as were the other band members.

At the end of the show, a D.J. started playing songs and women were grabbing at Travis to dance with them. He danced a few numbers and our host, who knew he was sick, rescued him.

We packed everything up and I went back to the RV to check on him. He looked horrible again. He was soaked with sweat and barely had the energy to get back on his feet. That night taught me a lot about the kind of entertainer he was. I had a lot of respect for him before, but that level of respect went up several notches that night. Fortunately, we have never faced an issue like that again.

In 2001 and 2002 we played several shows, including a few casinos and the county fair in Travis's hometown of Greenfield, Massachusetts.

Travis was the only Elvis act to perform at the Tupelo Elvis Festival in Elvis's hometown of Tupelo, Mississippi in 2000, 2001 and 2002. Travis did a small show there in 2000 and then became a headliner for the festival on June 1, 2001.

Dave Johnson Curt Werner Travis LeDoyt Dick McVey

That weekend he opened for Jerry Lee Lewis and on June 2, 2002 he opened for B. B. King and Charlie Daniels.

On July 4, 2002, we traveled to Arizona and opened a show for Little Richard at the Casino Del Sol in Tucson. After the Little Richard show, we asked if we could meet him. Our request made it up the chain of command and we were granted some time with him backstage. The rules were no autographs, no photos and keep it brief. I remember seeing a look of amazement on Richard's face when Travis walked into the room and his first words to Travis were, "I met Elvis back in the 50s and you're almost exactly like him."

Richard took time to greet each one of us and give us a hug. He also presented each one of us with a miniature booklet about Jesus and he warned Travis to avoid the temptations he would face in life and the problems that money could bring. It was a mini sermon about greed being the root of all evil. It was a great experience, and we were all surprised at how nice he treated us and disappointed that we couldn't get a photo or autograph.

In 2003, Travis had more memorable shows. He made his fourth consecutive appearance at the Tupelo Elvis Festival where we opened for Little Richard on June 7, 2003. The day before we were honored to open a show featuring Elvis's original band members D. J. Fontana and Scotty Moore. It was a thrill to see them play together at the festival. Another historic moment in our lives.

On June 26-28, 2003 Travis opened shows for Johnny Rivers at the Harrah's Cherokee Casino in Cherokee, North Carolina. An interesting story happened the first night there. Travis and the band had done their sound check and as Travis was leaving the stage Johnny Rivers asked Travis if he could borrow his guitar to do his sound check. Travis took off the guitar and handed it to Johnny and went to his room. Johnny told Travis he would have someone bring his guitar back to him after sound check, but that didn't happen. Travis went to Johnny's and when he knocked on the door Johnny was upset that Travis had disturbed him. Travis was trying to be nice, but Johnny grabbed the guitar, handed it to him and slammed the door. I had heard stories about Johnny being a little obnoxious and this incident confirmed those for me.

On August 2, 2003, Travis was invited to play the Oregon Jamboree opening for Alan Jackson, Ronnie Milsap and others. It was a huge festival in Sweet Home, Oregon featuring 15 of the nation's top country artists. The promoters had stumbled on Travis's promotional site and thought it might be a good diversion from all the country music and that strategy worked. Travis was well received and was asked to return on July 31, 2010 where he opened for Miranda Lambert and others. Miranda actually watched Travis's show before she went on and we found out she was telling people at other venues they should book him. It was very flattering coming from her as a fellow entertainer.

In 2004, Travis was contracted by Harrah's to perform 30 shows on Fridays and Saturdays throughout the year at their Tunica, Mississippi casino.

Travis was also contracted by Busch Gardens in Tampa, Florida to do a five-week series of shows. We performed on an open stage in the park and performed for more than 30,000 people during those five weeks. Our biggest issues at Busch Gardens were their rules and regulations. Right off the bat, they wanted the band to take drug tests and our upright bass player failed the test twice. It was a test where they cut a lock of hair that would show drug usage history for months back. I hired a second bass player and he too failed the test. It was getting close to time to sign the contracts and we didn't have a bass player, so I told Travis I would play bass. The problem was I couldn't do the first week because I had a recording session set up and couldn't get out of it. At the Rockabilly Festival in Jackson, Tennessee we had worked with Bill Haley's Comets and I had befriended Marshall Lytle, the original bass player who played on the hit, "Rock Around The Clock." I remembered Marshall telling me he lived in the Tampa area so I called to see if he could cover the first week of shows until I could get there. He agreed to do it and passed the drug test, as did I. Marshall played upright bass and was a master at the "slap bass" technique used on Elvis's early records so it was a perfect fit for the show. I arrived a week later and played bass the rest of our time there.

At the time the band was made up of Curt Werner on drums and Lin Poulson on guitar. We were also running backing tracks that included background vocals, piano, horns and strings. Curt ran the backing tracks from a CD player and that always worked fine, but in Tampa the stand they provided us for the CD player was a little wobbly and the tracks would skip sometimes. It was always funny when it happened because Curt would be in a panic trying to stop the CD player and Travis trying to act like nothing happened.

We did three shows a day, and I probably don't have to tell you it was hot in June in Tampa. The shows were short, normally 30-35 minutes so we had to cram as many hits in the show as we could. I think the shows were like 3 pm, 6 pm and 8 pm. We had access to the entire park so there were days we would go early and walk around and take in the rides and attractions. We had fans that started showing up at the shows every day. They were Tampa area residents who had annual passes, and nothing else to do. Of course, Travis's charisma both on and off stage won him thousands of new fans during that five-week period.

We had rented a three-bedroom apartment for our stay in Tampa, and I slept on the couch. Travis had a history of not sleeping well so we gave the room farthest away from everybody else and he covered the windows, so his room was pitch black. He had soundproofed it the best he could, so it was like a dark cave in there. Since we had a kitchen, we prepared some of our own meals, but after the shows we got into the bad habit of hitting the Steak & Shake almost every night.

During our time in Tampa, I met my future wife Charmaine and her family from Scotland. They were vacationing in Florida and came to our show. Charmaine became an instant Travis fan.

On October 23, 2004 we traveled to Canada for a show for one of the Elvis Fan Clubs there. Little did we know it would be our last show with guitarist Lin Poulson. Lin was one of those quiet guys who rarely said much, but when he spoke, he was funny and a great personality to have in the band. He had made a name for himself in Nashville playing hard-core traditional country music and rockabilly music. He had perfected Scotty Moore's guitar licks and sounds, and he stayed true to the music - a trait that Travis appreciated.

Less than two weeks later on November 3, 2004, I was working in my recording studio when I got a call from our drummer, Curt Werner. Curt asked me if I had heard a report that Steve Chapman had been killed in a car accident. Steve and Lin were great friends and Steve often went to shows and on road trips with us when his schedule allowed. Steve was a Tennessee State Trooper and was assigned to the security detail for Tennessee Governor, Phil Bredeson. I told Curt I didn't know anything about it, but I would call Lin and see if he knew anything. When I called Lin, his wife Kim answered and I asked, "Is this report true about Steve being killed in a car wreck?" Kim said, "You mean Steve and Lin?" and it knocked me back. I said, "Steve and Lin?" and she said, "Yes they were both killed. They're both gone." That news hit me like a ton of bricks. I felt so bad for calling Kim and I started apologizing and told her we would be there for her. She had visited Lin for a week when we were in Tampa, so we got to know her during that time.

Once I got off the phone with Kim, I called Travis and gave him the news. He was devastated, as was Curt when I called him back. It's hard to comprehend that someone who is like family is gone. It was a horrible feeling and time in our lives.

PHOTO BY DICK MCVEY

The accident happened on Election Day, November 2, 2004. Lin and Steve had been working at Steve's house rebuilding his back deck. Steve lived near Lebanon, Tennessee about 20 miles west of Nashville. He had to be downtown that evening because Governor Bredeson was having an election party. Steve was going to drop Lin off at his house and then go to the party. Just a few miles from Steve's house on a two-lane highway notorious for accidents there was a horrific accident. Since I've heard different versions of the details, I won't try to explain how it happened, but the results were tragic.

Mixed in with all the grief, I realized we had some big shows coming up and some big shoes to fill. I called my friend Penn Pennington, a multi-instrumentalist and he agreed to fill in for us until we could find someone. That's the great thing about Nashville - there is always a great musician just a phone call away.

On December 8, 2004 we headed out on our first big International Tour to China. We flew from Nashville to Detroit, Detroit to Tokyo and Tokyo to Hong Kong. The trip took us 26 hours total and we were exhausted. They couldn't get us seats together on the flight to Tokyo, so we were spread out all over this huge plane. I'm trying to sleep but I'm in the midst of a Japanese family of 14 people. I don't think they ever shut up. There would be no rest on the trip over.

I'm excited about this trip because we are going to be performing Christmas events for employees of a company called A. S. Watson and Company, who specialized in drinking water. On the show with us will be Gerry And The Pacemakers, Dan Seals, Jim Seals (from Seals & Crofts) and Mary Wilson and the Supremes.

As soon as we land in Hong Kong we are looking forward to a shower and a bed, but the promoter who greets us at the airport says. "We have big party for you tonight." Well, that's certainly not what we wanted to hear but we did get time for a shower and a couple of hours rest. The party was very cool and probably less than 50 people in attendance. Each act got up and performed a few songs, as did Travis. Getting to see and hear Gerry Marsden, lead singer of Gerry And The Pacemakers, was magic for me since that was one of the groups, I admired in the 60s. We actually used to do the songs "How Do You Do It" and "Ferry Across The Mersey" in my band back then. After the party there was a piano in the lobby and Travis, who is a marvelous pianist, was playing a few songs. Gerry asked Travis to play "Ferry Across The Mersey" while he sang it. That was a special night.

The next morning Penn and I decided to go have breakfast at the buffet in the Intercontinental Hotel and the array of food was incredible. The fruit in China seemed so much juicier and sweeter than in the US. One shock came when we got the bill for breakfast. It was over $500. Fortunately, the bill was in Hong Kong Dollars, so the real cost was about $30 each. It freaked us out for a second.

Later Travis and Curt joined us, and we walked into downtown Honk Kong. It was busy area, and people were constantly in your face selling things in the street, handing out advertising handbills for local restaurants and stores. Travis asked one of the girls handing out handbills if he could pass out a few. Of course, most people couldn't understand him, but Travis was putting on his best sales pitch out in the street. Even though Travis is not a sports fan, he was wearing a Boston Red Sox hat and he decided to try and sell it on the street. There were no buyers.

The Nashville agent, Judy Seale booked these shows and was with us on this tour. I had known Judy for a few years, and she had previously hired me to do some publicity work for The Bellamy Brothers. On this trip Judy gave us some special guide-lines for staying out of trouble. Since the SARS virus had hit China hard, there was a strict rule - no spitting on the street. A lot of people were wearing masks. The other big rule was not to take photographs of the older Chinese people. They believed the camera would capture their soul.

Judy flagged down a double decker bus and we made a complete loop of Hong Kong. It seemed odd to see places like Kentucky Fried Chicken and Burger King but there were lots of American and British stores and restaurants, especially in Hong Kong. We climbed to the top of the bus and I had my video camera rolling as we made our run around the city. There were massive tall apartment complexes and every balcony was draped with clothes drying. The air was very dirty, and Travis remarked that the clothing hanging out to dry must smell hor-rible. There were thousands of taxis and motorcycles in the streets, but very few private cars. There were buildings and smog as far as the eye could see.

At the end of the bus tour, Travis told Judy he would like to see about getting a custom suit made while he was there. Judy had some connections and took Travis to a tailor where Travis picked out the style of suit he wanted and the material. The next day the suit was finished and fit Travis perfectly.

The following day we left Hong Kong and headed into Com-munist China. For a hillbilly who grew up during the Cold War, the word "Communist" always got my attention, so for me this was like driving into the land of the enemy. When we arrived at the border between Hong Kong and China, we had to go through an Immigration process. In that area no cameras are allowed but since I didn't see the sign, I am taking pictures. Travis told me cameras were not allowed but I thought he was joking so

I kept snapping. Then a soldier with a machine gun came over pointing at my camera and shaking his head "no". I was afraid he would take the camera but once I put it away, he moved back to his post. I will tell you he kept a close watch on me after that. They had me stand on a small podium and they fired a thermal beam at me that read my temperature. They had warned us that if anyone had a temperature they would not be allowed into Communist China.

Once we did all our paperwork and our bus was allowed to go through, the driving lanes changed from driving on the left to driving on the right. By that I mean in Hong Kong you drive on the left side of the road like if you were in England. Once you cross into China you drive on the right side of the road like we do here in the U.S. It has to be a little confusing for the drivers, but I guess they are used to the change.

As we drove through Communist China, it didn't look much different than it does driving through the U. S., including lots of American stores like Walmart. It was a little shocking but in reality, a number of the stores and restaurants you see in the world bear American trademark signs.

Our next show is in Shenzhen, China. We arrived in the early afternoon at the Crowne Plaza Hotel. That doesn't sound Chinese does it? The hotel is a tall high rise similar to the one in Hong Kong. It is very elaborate, and everything is first class. The language barrier is worse than in Hong Kong and we found very few people that could speak English so ordering food was difficult. I pointed at what I wanted on the menu and still didn't know exactly what I would be getting.

The following night we had our first show in Shenzhen and we were doing two shows with an intermission. The audience was very polite, unlike the craziness we had seen with fans in Hong Kong. Between sets Travis was asking the promoter if the audiences were always so subdued. The promoter laughed and said, "You have to give them your permission to be loud, otherwise you will only get polite applause at the end of each song." Before the promoter introduced the second set, he told the audience in Chinese that Travis wanted them to have fun and dance if they wanted. The next set was a totally different audience once Travis gave them his approval to get wild. The audience was up dancing and clapping and their polite applause turned energetic and there were lots of screams and whistles. It was interesting witnessing the change.

Oddly enough, the theme of the evening was "Cowboys and Indians" and everyone was dressed as a cowboy or an Indian. I don't know if it was intentional or not but some were dressed as East Indians, instead of American Indians.

Our rooms were on one of the top floors in the hotel and you could go on the balcony and see as far as the smog would allow. The cityscape was much like that of Hong Kong with hundreds of apartment buildings and again, lots of clothes hanging off the balconies to dry. The craziest thing was a theme park across the street called "Happy Valley" that was very similar to Disneyland. From our vantage point we could see the layout of the park and Travis and I were commenting that this section looked like Adventureland, and this section looked like Main Street and so on. It was interesting and definitely something we will never forget.

The following day Judy had arranged for two bodyguards to take us to a shopping area set up like a flea market. The booths were in a building that looked like a parking garage that was several floors high. Each level had rows of cubicles that were about 8 feet by 8 feet and each cubicle had its own display of products. There was everything there you could imagine. As Americans, we stood about 6" taller than the locals and that coupled with the way we dressed made us marks for merchants who had the idea that all Americans were rich. Our two bodyguards had warned us there would be pick pockets and that merchants would be grabbing at us to come and look at what they were selling. Whenever one of the locals would grab us, one of the bodyguards would say something to them in Chinese and they would back off. There were lots of knock-off items and if we saw something we were interested in, one of the bodyguards would check it out for us. Most of the electronics and watches were fake. I bought two Rolex watches knowing they were knock offs but they looked so good I couldn't resist.

The place was quite dirty and there was a lot of traffic. I moved my wallet to my front pocket and kept my hand on it most of the time I was there. As I turned one corner there was a Dentist pulling a tooth in quite unsanitary conditions with people watching just a few feet from the patient. It was strange for sure.

As we finished our day of shopping and went down to the area to get our taxis back to the hotel, there were about two dozen handicapped people dragging themselves on the dirty floor from one person to the next begging for money. It was not how I wanted to end my day, and I have thought about those people many times since.

The next morning, we headed back to Hong Kong and the trip was uneventful. When we arrived at Immigration, I did not take out my camera. I wanted to make sure I didn't jeopardize my trip home the next day. My temperature was normal so there were no issues getting back into Hong Kong and it was smooth sailing back to the USA.

Our next show was at Mystic Lake Casino in Prior Lake, Minnesota so we flew from China to Minneapolis. We got to the venue pretty beat up. Long flights, jet lag and the crazy time differences. At noon in Minnesota, it would be 1 am in Hong Kong so it totally flipped our body clock around.

The casino show was Christmas themed and the entertainment director had hired Las Vegas dancers to enhance our show. They were scantily clad and their boss, who was a lady, was very proud of her girls. She talked about them up at every opportunity bragging about their beauty and how well they danced. Of course, the show required extra rehearsal time so we spent most of the afternoon on stage and we were all a little tired and grumpy. After rehearsal we made plans to eat and when we went to the dining room, the girls and their boss were already seated at a table. They have seats for us and guided us to the table so the only polite thing to do was sit down. The meal was really nice and the mood at the table was lighthearted and enjoyable - except for the boss lady continuing her never-ending praise of her girls. I hadn't been talking much because when I'm tired, I'm usually quiet. At one point the boss lady said to me, "You know you haven't said much about my girls. I saw you looking at them." I looked at her and said, "You know what. I'd rather see a big piece of prime rib." She didn't speak to me for the next four days and I loved it.

At the end of our run at Mystic Lake Casino, we flew home from Minneapolis on Southwest Airlines. At Southwest you do not have reserved seats and you can sit anywhere on the plane. If you're one of the first people on board you can pick most any seat. When flying on Southwest, Travis always had a strategy. He would take a window seat and I would take the aisle seat. We would always ignore people as they came by hoping the middle seat would remain open and give us a little more room. We would always ask the flight attendant if the plane was going to be full and, on this day, she said there were only going to be about three vacant seats. We were trying to figure out how we could keep that middle seat to ourselves. Travis was wearing a pretty heavy jacket and a baseball cap and he took off the jacket and wrapped it around his arm and put the baseball cap on top of his hand. He leaned over to the middle seat and it looked like a little kid was sitting there. If someone came by, Travis would lean over and act like he was talking to this imaginery kid. People just kept passing by, but no one realized it was a dummy. The flight attendant said it was genius.

There was another occasion when Travis took off his shirt. No one sat beside him that day either.

We began 2005 with doing a couple of concerts to commemorate the 50th anniversary of Elvis's 1955 tour. We played venues in Helena, Arkansas and New Boston, Texas where Elvis actually played in 1955, fifty years before.

We also hired Dave Johnson on guitar and he started working with us on May 13, 2005 at the Harrah's Ak-Chin Casino in Maricopa, Arizona about 40 miles south of Phoenix. We had flown into Phoenix and rented a van to make the commute back and forth to the casino from our hotel in Phoenix. For some reason we never stayed at the hotel at the casino and I suspected that hotel stayed full year-round. Dave had gone swimming sometime during the day and he had hung his wet swimming trunks on the van to dry so when we left to go to the casino, he walked over to the van to get his trunks when he realized he had put them on the wrong van. Dave was always a good sport and he was so easy going that Travis would pull pranks on him when he could. Dave would never admit he had been pranked which was his way of getting back at Travis. He didn't want Travis to have the satisfaction of knowing he "got him."

After Harrah's we did two weeks in Elko, Nevada at the Red Lion Inn and Casino. It was a good opportunity to work with Dave and learn more songs to break him in to the band. It was a beautiful area, but after two weeks we were ready to head home.

We played at the Tupelo Elvis Festival again on the weekend of June 3, 2005 and it would be a memorable weekend because we would be opening the big stage show for Chuck Berry. Chuck had made quite an entrance as he arrived in Tupelo. He was driving an RV and nearly took out a brick building and narrowly missed hitting a festival worker.

Chuck's contract stated that the Festival would provide him a backup band, but when Chuck arrived, he had his own band with him. He called the Festival bigwigs to his RV telling them he was going to use his own band and the Festival was going to have to pay them. This set off a series of events that lasted three hours. Chuck refused to go on stage and the Festival refused to pay the extra musicians so it became a stalemate. In my years being around concert promoters, I had heard similar stories about Chuck showing up and demanding extra money for this and that so I wasn't too surprised with what was happening.

As the festival managers continued negotiations with Chuck in his RV backstage, it was time for Travis to take the stage. A Festival representative came over and told us to go on stage and play until they could either get Chuck to play or announce he wouldn't be performing. I was having flashbacks to my days opening for Jerry Lee Lewis when similar things happened and I was designated to tell the audience the star of the show wasn't going to show. Not fun.

There were thousands of people in the audience and Travis got a rousing welcome. We had a planned show, but when we finished what should have been our final song, a Festival rep came to me and said keep playing so we did. Obviously, I'm thinking negotiations in the RV are not going well.

About that time, I heard a roar from the audience and I looked over and here comes Chuck up the steps to the stage. He's got his guitar around his neck and it looks to me like to me he's coming to play. I don't remember what song we were doing but I started thinking he's going to jump up here and play with us. I'm going to get to play with Chuck Berry. His band was nowhere in sight so why would he come on stage if he wasn't going to play. When he got onstage and right in the middle of Travis's show he grabs the microphone. We stopped playing and he says (over the microphone so everyone can hear), "You're done. It's my turn now."

We were shocked and immediately started getting our stuff off the stage. Chuck wasn't happy and since he had to wait for his band to get on stage he just stood there. His show wasn't great, his guitar was out of tune, the band was average at best but, as he did that famous "duck walk" across the stage, I just said to myself, you know that's Chuck Berry. Another cool "bucket list" moment in my life.

That weekend we also did the Sunday Gospel Show as a part of the festival and the response to that show was incredible and became a regular part of the weekend. It was a long hot summer and we had big shows on June 9, 2005 at Hershey Park in Pennsylvania and on August 5, 2005 we played the International Hot Rod Association Convention at Freedom Hall in Louisville, Kentucky.

As summer faded, we were scheduled to do a show on November 25, 2005, at Fort Randall Casino in Pickstown, South Dakota. Weather is always a concern anytime you're going to South Dakota in the winter months and we arrived just ahead of a snowstorm.

It took us 18 hours to drive there but we got some much-needed rest. We slept in, had lunch and went over to the show room for our sound check. Once we finished with sound check, there was a lady sitting toward the back of the room near the bar. As we walked by, she reached out and grabbed Travis by the arm and said, "You are absolutely the worst Elvis I have ever seen." She was obviously drunk, but Travis politely said, "Thank you." She said, "I don't think you understood me, you are the worst Elvis I have ever seen." Travis again repeated, "Thank you ma'am." As we exited the conversation continues with Travis always being polite and thanking her. Travis continued making it sound like she was a giving him a compliment. We were concerned that she would be there for the show and cause more trouble but the show didn't happen.

Around 5 pm I got a call from Herb Hare, the entertainment director at the time and I could hear the concern in his voice. He said, "Dick if you boys want to get home you need to leave now. This storm is moving faster than they expected and it's going to be here in a few hours. I don't want you to be stuck here for a few days." I called the guys and we headed down to the showroom to tear down.

Curt Werner was our drummer. He was born and raised in Minnesota so he was our go-to driver in bad weather. By the time we got to the van and trailer they were coated with about an inch of ice. We started the process of getting in the driver's side door so we could start the van and get some heat going to help melt the ice on the windows and have the ability to open the other doors. The van and trailer probably weighed twice as much as it would normally. We left the van running and began the process of trying to get the trailer door open, which took about 15 minutes. We had everything ready to go so we loaded the trailer and I went back to my room to get my suitcase. There was literally no one in the casino except us and a few employees. We knocked some more ice off the van and trailer and Curt started driving a route to get us out of the path of the storm. That took about 3 hours of treacherous roads but we made it. It was good to get back to Nashville alive.

At the end of the year, we had shows at Harrah's Rincon Casino near San Diego, California on December 29 & 30, 2005. From there we flew to Albuquerque, New Mexico and then had to drive three hours north for a New Year's Eve show at a theater in Farmington, New Mexico. When we landed in Albuquerque, Travis's luggage did not arrive. We waited until they located his bags but they were still in San Diego. He didn't have any stage clothes or shoes. We had to start driving in order to get to Farmington on time so off we went, trying to decide what we could do for stage clothes for Travis. Fortunately, in the 50s, Elvis often wore black pants and standard long sleeve shirts so we figured a quick run to Walmart would solve the problem when we got to Farmington.

We called the theater with our dilemma, so when we arrived, they had an employee waiting to whisk Travis away to get some clothes. We got the stage set up and did the sound check without Travis. Showtime was coming up fast and Travis wasn't back yet. We knew it shouldn't have taken so long and now the theater manager is starting to get antsy, and so am I.

It's about 10 minutes to showtime when Travis pops through the back door and starts scrambling to get dressed. I asked him, "What took so long?" He said, "We went to Walmart but they got a bomb threat so everybody had to leave. We went to Kmart but it was farther away."

The band took the stage and I looked over just before I introduced him and he's sitting on the side of the stage tying his shoes. The show went off on time, but that is the closest call we ever had for starting a show late.

Following the show, I went to the manager's office to get paid and she was drunk as a skunk. I never did figure out if it was because it was New Year's Eve or if she was so stressed, she needed some relief. We talked for a few minutes as she wrote out our check, and she was slurring her words and her writing was very impaired. I could barely read the check. Earlier in the day she had introduced me to her boyfriend so I went to him and told him I needed him to write the check and just have her sign it. He looked at the check and chuckled, agreeing that it was a mess. I'm glad he was there and we were able to get a check our bank would accept.

On February 6, 2006 we played at the Averitt Performing Arts Center in Statesboro, Georgia. They put us up in a beautiful Bed and Breakfast that had themed rooms decorated in the colors and with paintings representing each theme. Even the throw rugs were color coordinated to each room. Travis thought it would be funny to change the theme from one room to another so as to confuse the maids when they came to clean. Travis determined the red themed room should be blue and the blue themed room should be yellow. A sign on the designated the theme of each room, so it must have been an interesting morning after we checked out. We never heard anything about our antics, but we never played the Averitt Performing Arts Center again.

In addition to running all over the U.S. we made two visits to England in 2006. The first trip was the result of Charmaine writing a positive review about Travis that was seen by a show promoter in England. The promoter asked Charmaine if she thought Travis would be a hit in the UK and she gave us rave reviews. That sealed the deal for us to play the Americana Festival on July 8-9, 2006 at the Newark Showgrounds near Nottingham. Travis was greeted by an enthusiastic audience of 15,000 people and the scene was like the real Elvis was on stage. Offstage after the show it was near pandemonium with people wanting to buy his merchandise and get photos with him. The show was such a success that the pro-moter decided to have Travis come back for a three-week tour starting on October 11, 2006. That tour would take us all across England and to Edinburgh, Scotland, where Charmaine actually promoted a sold-out show in her hometown.

She did the show as a benefit for her sister-in-law who had cancer and the response was overwhelming. I remember that night vividly and I really thought Charmaine was a beautiful person. Then I met her husband and that killed any ideas I might have had.

We were traveling nearly every day in a van. It was tiring, but we were all able to catch a few winks as we traveled up and down the road. In the U.S. it was not uncommon to jump in the van and travel 15-18 hours to get to a show. In England, they seemed to think a 3-hour trip was an impossible task. If we had to go more than 3 hours, the driver would start looking for a motel to sleep a few hours and then get up early and finish the trip. It was very uncharacteristic for us since we would finish the entire trip and then sleep. At any rate it was a quirky thing and we quickly came to expect two short trips instead of one long one. The driver insisted he couldn't do it and who were we to argue the point. Our lives were in his hands.

Typically, when we arrived at a motel, I would get out, check us in, sign all the paperwork and get the room keys. The other band members and Travis unloaded our suitcases and equip-ment. One day I got quite a surprise. I was riding in the front seat and Travis was behind me. I had been sleeping and when we pulled into the motel, Travis woke me up and told me we had arrived. I got out and went to the front desk and was checking us in, and, as usual the band started bringing our luggage and in-struments into the lobby. I had on a baseball cap and when I bent over for something, a big blob of shaving cream fell off the top of my head. As we were riding, Travis was putting on layer after layer of shaving cream on my head and no one told me - not even the girl at the front desk.

When we got to Scotland, we stayed in an old hotel there

that was quite ornate and each room had its own interesting decor. I had bought a video camera and I was filming the inside of my room when I got a call from Travis inviting me over to check out his room. I took my camera and filmed my trip down the hall to his room. The camera was still rolling when I got there and knocked on his door. He answered the door stark naked. I acted as if nothing was wrong and continued to film as he gave me a full tour of his room in the buff. I never acknowledged the fact that he was naked and he didn't either. Part of the fun of our pranks and jokes was that neither would acknowledge anything happened and try and remain straight-faced as they happened.

Traveling through England and Scotland was a treat other than the chilly and cloudy weather. It rained or snowed on all of but three days we were there. We were told that the dismal weather there contributes to their high suicide rate. Toward the end of that tour, we all knew why.

There was beautiful countryside and scenery and we made a lot of interesting stops along the way. When we were off the road we were headquartered in Nottingham, near Nottingham Castle and Sherwood Forest - yes, they really exist. In front of the castle is a statue of Robin Hood and just down the street is the "Ye Olde Trip to Jerusalem," a pub that dates back to 1189. There was also a wonderful art museum near the castle where we fit in like a fish out of water. As my Mom would say, there were a lot of "snooty" people there. They were very well dressed. We arrived in blue jeans, t-shirts and I was wearing a "Country Music Television" jacket. I would venture a guess that a CMT jacket had never been worn in this building before or since.

Some of the paintings were truly remarkable and some of them covered the entire side of a room, I'm guessing around 15' by 30'. Travis and I stood there gawking as these rare paintings and I said to Travis, "That would look really nice in your living room." At about that time a museum worker walked by and, without looking up from his clipboard, and in a very posh English accent said, "I don't think so."

As we were driving through the English countryside, somebody excitedly asked our driver, "Hey, is that Stonehenge over there?" The driver said, "Yes, it is." I asked, "Can we stop?" The driver said, "We don't have time to stop today, but we will stop tomorrow on our way to the next show." I was more than concerned he was just saying that and I would miss this opportunity to visit a "bucket list" site.

The next day, the driver held to his promise and, we did indeed stop and spent a few hours hanging out there. Needless to say, I took a lot of photos and we walked around, admiring the structure and letting our imaginations run wild as to how it got there. There was a wonderful museum where we got a lot of answers, but Stonehenge is one of those places where I somehow feel drawn. Charmaine and I traveled there again in 2016 and they had made quite a few changes in how you enter the area and there was more flexibility to walk completely around the stones.

We also spent a day in London where we visited Big Ben, The Houses Of Parliament, Westminster Abbey, The Tower Of London, The Tower Bridge, and Buckingham Palace. It was another one of those days that was damp and chilly but since we had a lot to see the day went by rather quickly. We also got to experience the London Underground subway system and that was an experience in itself. It was extremely crowded and the people riding had short tempers.

The tour overall was a good experience, but the promoter made promises he couldn't keep and was in over his head. He had promoted single shows successfully, but he had never taken an act on a multi-city tour. Playing three or four days a week in different towns just overwhelmed him. There were a lot of logistic problems and multi-city promotion is a lot of hard work and normally handled by several people as a full-time job. He was a great guy but he got in too deep with this tour. About half the dates were great, but the other half were not well attended and some were held in local pubs rather than theaters as he had promised.

One of the clubs we played was called MFN and it stood for "middle of f'n nowhere." Another city we played had no motel and we had to take cold showers upstairs near the pub office. They had no hot running water. A couple of places I would describe as "biker bars" and once we started a show a lot of people left the building. Those venues were a total mismatch for us and the promoter should have known that. I think he promised us a lot of shows and, when he couldn't get the right venues for us, he started taking what he could get. A lot of things that were promised in the contract were not fulfilled and we ended up footing the bill for nearly $300 worth of food that he was supposed to provide. On our final day, we had a late-night flight back to the U.S. The promoter and his wife / business partner picked us up at the motel and they were yelling at each other as we got in the car. She had had a few drinks was complaining about money and the fact that the tour hadn't met her financial expectations. She was smoking a cigarette and the promoter asked her several times to put it out because Travis has problems with the smoke. She kept smoking and the third time he asked her he smacked the cigarette out of her mouth. She went to light another and he smacked it down. Her next statement was she wasn't going to pay us since the tour did poorly, and they went at it. All this time he is driving us to the airport and most of the time I saw the speedometer over 100 miles per hour and as high as 115.

As we neared the airport she reached into her bag and gave me a bag of cash. I didn't have time to count it all since it was smaller bills. She said, "You don't have to count it, it's all there." Once we got in the airport, Travis and I counted it and sure enough she paid us in U.S. currency what they owed minus the bill for food, that we never got. Needless to say, we never worked with them again, and it was a shame that she blamed us for their lack of promotion.

After that we played England a few times including the Hemsby Festival and an annual holiday show in Lowestoft for two different promoters. The Festivals were geared for a "rockabilly" crowd and the people dressed 50s style and the bands all had upright bass players with tattoos - except us. The people at those "rockabilly "shows did not like me because I didn't play an upright bass. At one point it got nasty with people yelling at me. One guy was yelling to Travis, "Get a proper bass player." The magazines there would give Travis rave reviews but they always criticized the band. On writer said the band was "too perfect." I never quite figured that one out. When all was said and done, the band stopped going and Travis worked with the bands there.

On our last show in the United Kingdom, we almost didn't get home. There had just been a rash of airline pilots in the news being fired for drinking, so when the pilots for our flight came by us to board the plane, I thought it would be funny to make a joke. I said, "I sure hope you guys haven't been drinking." The pilot turned and gave me a "look" but kept walking. Then I said, "He must be hung over." He stopped in his tracks and came back to where we were sitting. He asked, "Are you on this flight?" I said, "Yes sir." He said, "Do you realize I am the Captain of this flight?" I replied, "Yes sir." He asked. "Do you understand that I have the authority to keep you from boarding this flight?" Again, I replied, "Yes sir." He said, "Well, I suggest you keep your smart-ass remarks to yourself. Do you understand?" I said, "Yes sir, I'm sorry." He walked away, but the band started making fun of how somebody had found a way to shut my sarcastic mouth. Believe me, I really wanted to be on that flight so I was quiet as a mouse after that.

On April 7, 2007, we played a festival in northern Scotland. Our flights took us in and out of Inverness and it was another two-hour trip to Thurso, one of the northernmost parts of Scotland. It was a beautiful drive and once we arrived the view from our hotel room was incredible. I wish I had my Nikon camera on this trip because we saw some amazing things. This was the first year Charmaine and I had been together and it felt really strange that I was in her home country of Scotland while she was in Nashville. The communications at the hotel were primitive and required the switchboard operator to place calls for the guests. We got there on Charmaine's birthday, April 6, 2007 and I was trying desperately to call her. Because of the time difference I decided to wait until 2 am in Scotland which was 8 pm in Nashville. Obviously, the hotel wasn't used to having a lot of people needing to make calls at that time of night and there was only person at the hotel desk. He was the only person who could place a call - and he was drunk. Charmaine was trying to call me and I was trying to call her but this old gentleman trying to run the switchboard had no idea how to connect an international telephone call. It was a frustrating evening, but I was able to get a call through the next day and Charmaine and I laughed at some of things the frustrated old man said that can't be repeated here.

Our show went very well and the next day we were treated to a VIP tour of the Queen Mother's Castle of Mey in Caithness. The person giving us the tour worked for the Queen Mother (Queen Elizabeth's mother) until her death and he had been placed in charge of the Castle. It was closed to the public the day we were there so we got to see a lot of things that were off limits to tourists, and we got a lot of inside information about the Royal Family and what it was like to be in that circle of people. The grounds were huge and we spent several hours walking around. In the garden there was a tree that had been planted by Prince Charles and Lady Diana as a memorial to the Queen Mother.

That night we had to leave for the airport at around 10 pm for a 3 am flight to London. When traveling in Scotland we often heard the Scots talk about how they didn't like the English and their disdain for the way England was trying to run things in the UK. Travis had picked up on a lot of the "trash talk" by the Scots so when we boarded the plane and just before takeoff, Travis said, in a loud voice, "The English think they're better than the Scots and it just makes me sick." If there was a quiet time on a plane before takeoff, Travis would often blurt out, "Boring" stretching the word out to make it as long as he could.

In 2010, I got a call from a friend of mine telling me I needed to go see an act named Brandon Giles who was playing down-town on Broadway in Nashville. Brandon was a wild and crazy entertainer who could mimic Jerry Lee Lewis. After several conversations with Brandon, I told him if he would be willing to do Jerry Lee Lewis, I thought I could pair him up with Travis and maybe even do a "Million Dollar Quartet" style show.

It wasn't long after that a show came up at the Carson Center in Paducah, Kentucky where a promoter wanted to put a show together and produce a "Million Dollar Quartet" show, so I booked Travis as Elvis and Brandon as Jerry Lee on the show.

Brandon had been doing his own thing for a while but agreed to be Jerry Lee on this night. Brandon had a great guitar player but he had a modern, even heavy metal sound. Brandon agreed to talk with him and get him settled down for this particular show. I was concerned but Brandon was a professional so I expected him to handle it. He didn't. At sound check the guitar was playing extremely loud and nothing that resembled a 50s style. It was more like Van Halen. I went to the stage several times during sound check and even though I assured the promoter everything would be alright; I had a bad feeling.

As Brandon hit the stage, he was a full-on showman. He played the piano with his feet, his rear and then he stood up on the piano and set it on fire. I was standing there with the promoter and he asked me if I knew Brandon was going to do that. Before I could answer, the Fire Marshal (who happened to be attending the show) came running backstage screaming that we needed to get him off stage.

Since the piano burning was the grand finale (and the crowd

loved it by the way), Brandon came off stage where the Fire Marshal promptly threatened to arrest him – and me. It took some talking but I finally got the Fire Marshal settled down and explained I specifically told Brandon not to do that. This was a fairly new building so they were more-than-concerned about seeing it go up in smoke. After the show, I saw Brandon in the lobby and ended our brief but eventful relationship. Travis had done an exceptional show and that seemed to settle down the promoter. I apologized over and over to the promoter for the guitarist and the fire and let him know I would no longer be affiliated with Brandon.

We had done a show in Travis's hometown of Greenfield, Massachusetts and the following day we were flying back to Nashville from Hartford, Connecticut. We spent three days in Greenfield and the band stayed with Dr. Russ Thomas and his wife Sandy who always hosted us when we played there. We got to the airport and as we are going through security, the TSA grabbed Curt Werner's carry-on bag and pulled it to the side. They sent an additional officer to escort Curt to a secure area. We often had bags searched and there was usually no problem, but today the TSA officer reached into Curt's bag and pulled out the longest pair of scissors I have ever seen. Obviously, Curt hadn't brought them with him or they would have been found flying out of Nashville. We all immediately looked at Travis, who continues to this day to deny he planted those scissors, and to this day we all think he did.

Over the years I saw many snafus with equipment, where a sound company who was supposed to be providing equipment brought the wrong equipment or left key elements of an instrument back at their shop which made the equipment unusable. They would forget things like power cords and speaker cords. They would forget to bring the drum seat or throne, a snare stand, a piece of the hi-hat or kick drum pedal. It wasn't a common thing but it did happen and either they would be able to source something at a local music store or we would figure a way to work around it.

DAVE JOHNSON   STEVE UNDERWOOD   DICK MCVEY

On June 15, 2014 we were set to play an outdoor show at St. Jo Frontier Casino in St. Joseph, Missouri. The sound and lighting company was on the scene and everything looked great - except there was no drum seat (throne). Steve Underwood, our drummer at the time, was a seasoned show veteran who had worked with Vern Gosdin and a number of country music artists, so he had seen just about everything and he had the solution. A folding chair with a road case on top of it situated caddy corner on the chair. He cautioned us that at some point in the show he may fall off the back of the stage, but to keep playing and he would be back as soon as he could.

The biggest mistake I ever made booking Travis happened November 21, 2015. We were scheduled for a show in Powhatten, Kansas at the Sac & Fox Casino and, like many of the Indian-owned casinos, it was in a remote area about 60 miles north of Topeka. We arrived the night before and got a good night's sleep and headed to lunch at noon and then over to the showroom. Our show was in conjunction with a car show and there was a lot of activity inside the casino and in the parking lot. As we went to the showroom, I could hear someone making announcements over a PA system, and the person who booked us was running all over the place trying to make sure all the events were running smoothly.

Normally when we walk into a showroom for our soundcheck, the sound and light crew are already on the scene and the PA or sound system and lighting are all in place. This time was different. There was no sound system and I remember being really irritated because this meant we were going to have to wait on them to set up and that often took hours.

About that time the entertainment director came in and I asked what time the sound company would be coming. He looked at me with a strange look and said, "You were supposed to supply the sound system." My stomach flipped and I felt a large dose of adrenalin race through my body. I asked, "Are you sure?" and he said, "Yes it's in the contract." In disbelief I looked at a copy of the contract I had on my phone and sure enough, we were supposed to provide the sound system. In a panicked state, I confessed I had screwed up and asked if there was a music store close by, or if there was somewhere we could rent a system. He replied there wasn't anyone nearby that could get the equipment to us in time. He was not happy and I was embarrassed and trying to figure out what we could do. I asked about the sound system I had heard in the parking lot earlier and he said that was brought in by the car show and they would be using it all day.

It's about 2:30 pm and the show is at 7 pm. I kept reassuring Travis we'd figure something out and make it work. The entertainment director said that sometimes the sound company he used would leave equipment in a back room and we rushed to see if we could be so lucky. The good news was there were cables, power amps and speakers. The bad news there was no reverb unit or soundboard to mix the sound. Travis remembered he had a tiny 4-channel mixer under the seat in the van. Normally we need at least 16 channels to mix a show, but at that point I am so happy that we will be able to do the show - not like we want to but we can pull off something. Travis carried his own microphone and the casino found a few more so we put a microphone on the bass drum, one on the snare, one microphone overhead to capture the drums and one for Travis's vocal. Somehow it worked.

It had been years since we had to provide our own sound for a show and it's one of those times where I didn't look at the contract before the show. That doesn't happen any longer. Fortunately, we had a good, receptive crowd and I don't think anyone in the audience knew the difference. Unfortunately, the entertainment director was more than unhappy with me and rightfully so. He never asked us to play there again.

Our next gig was playing the Lucky Eagle Casino in Rochester, Washington. We got there the night before and checked in to the casino hotel. The next day went down for lunch and on our way back to the room Travis stopped by the front desk and asked the girl if anybody had ever reported any paranormal activity in his room. The girl said no, but she called another girl up to the desk and asked her and she started telling a ghost story. Travis looked surprised and told them he had seen that same thing in his room the night before. They were spooked out and Travis embellished his version of the ghost. The girls summoned the female manager and I thought Travis would back away and tell them it was a joke, but no. He starts telling this manager of his scary night.

A lot of times the people at the hotel don't know us or what we were doing at the casino. When one of the girls remarked that Travis looked like Elvis, he let them know we were doing a show in the casino. They asked him what songs he might be doing and he told them he didn't sing. He told them he would be reading poetry. Again, I thought he would tell them the truth, but he didn't. I often wonder what they thought after they heard people talking about the show later on.

Travis and I also do a bit where we get on the elevator with other people and he or I will make up a story. It's a form of improv and I don't think we've ever done it without success. Some examples are we would get on the elevator and out of the blue Travis would say, "Did they get that lizard out of your room?" and I would play along. Before long people on the elevator would start asking questions to which we lied our asses off. Once I asked Travis, "What's going on with all that money you found in your room?" Travis would say he turned it in at the front desk. Then people would start asking how much money and why did you turn it in and all kinds of fun questions. Depending on the age of the people, the subject may be a little more adult like Travis would say, "Hey did you get that problem taken care of?" I would reply "Yes, but I'm still not able to pee normally." The replies and responses would vary depending on what the other people said, but I don't remember them responding to that one. They would squirm and move away from me though.

Some of my favorite pranks were ones Travis played on guitar player Dave Johnson. Travis had a way of getting our room keys and while we were out, he would trash our rooms or play pranks. One night we were playing a casino up north in the winter and there was about a foot of snow on our balconies. We each had our own room but there were two beds in each room. Travis got Dave's room key, went on the balcony and scooped up about three hands full of snow and dumped them into the bed Dave had slept in the night before. He put the snow under the covers and left.

The next day we're all waiting for Dave to say something, but he never did. We played the shows and left the next day, and Dave still hasn't mentioned the snow. So, Travis casually asks, "How did everybody sleep last night?" And Dave says, "Well you know that bed I slept in the first night hurt my back so last night I slept in the other bed and it was really good." Dave had figured a way to avoid being the brunt of the joke but we all knew what happened. That got a good laugh.

I think the best prank Travis ever played was on Dave Johnson was on a road trip in the van. We had stopped for gas and Travis and I got back to the car before anyone else and Travis saw that Dave had left his cell phone. This was before phones could be locked and Travis grabbed his phone. He quickly exchanged his number for Dave's wife's number so that when he sent a text to Dave's phone it would look like it was coming from Dave's wife Anita. We had been working together for so long that we all knew each other's wives and their habits and we also knew what would push each other's buttons. Such was the case with Anita who had a love for animals and would rescue dogs and cats and take them home.

Dave was sitting in the front passenger seat and Travis was directly behind him. I was driving at the time. A few miles down the road Dave's phone lit up with a message from "Anita" but it was actually Travis. Dave read the message and immediately started whining and said, "Oh Anita." I asked him what she said and he said, "Well she's found this dog on the side of the road and wants to take it home." He didn't answer her right away because he wasn't sure how he was going to handle it, but he started moaning to us. He went on and on like "I'm just going to have to tell her that we can't have another dog and she's going to have to stop picking up animals like this." We're all trying to tell him how he could probably make room for one more dog, especially if she thought this was a "keeper."

He finally sent a reply saying he didn't think it was a good idea and she should start looking for the owner or trying to find a home for the dog. Travis responded and the texting went back and forth for about 30 minutes. "Anita" (Travis) kept insisting they keep the dog and Dave fighting it as diplomatically as he could.

After a bit, "Anita" got home and when she went into the house, she told Dave the roof was leaking in his studio and some of his equipment had gotten damaged. That's when he decided he'd better call "Anita" which rang Travis's phone and the cat (or dog) was out of the bag. We laughed for the longest time and even Dave agreed it was a "good one".

For a period of time my wife, Charmaine would travel with us on the road and after nearly every meal, Travis found a way to get silverware or salt and pepper shakers in her purse or coat pocket. One time he filled my pockets with raw broccoli from a deli tray backstage.

The best prank he played on Charmaine and me was at the Hard Rock Hotel in Tulsa. After we did the show and had dinner, Charmaine and I decided we would gamble a little before going back to our room. Travis stopped by the front desk and got a key to our room and when  we returned our mattress and box springs were missing. It was obvious where they might be, so we went to his room and knocked on the door. There was no answer. We tried to call the room and Travis's cellphone and no answer. It was clear this wasn't a one-man job, so Dave Johnson came to mind. Dave was not good at lying and if he played a joke on you or lied to you, he would soon admit it, and his admission would always start with the phrase, "I gotta level with you."

I called Dave's cellphone and he answered. I said, "Where are you?" and he answered, "I'm in Travis's room." I just said, "OK, I'm coming over." This time when I knocked, Dave answered the door. I said, "Do you know what happened to our mattress?" Dave just pointed toward Travis's bed, and there was Travis laying on his bed and our bed stacked on top of it. He was about 6 feet in the air, laying there like a king and not acknowledging that anything was wrong. After a few minutes, he and Dave put our bed back in our room. That was not the end of the story.

The next day, we were running a little late and Travis asked Charmaine if she could iron his clothes while we did a sound check. He gave her the key to his room and she ironed his clothes but she also rolled toilet paper all over the room and rearranged as much of the room as she could and hid his towels. It was a grand act of revenge.

Dave was an easygoing guy, but there was an incident at a motel where the maid kept knocking on his door while he had the "Do Not Disturb" sign out. The first time he let it go, the second time he explained to her that if his sign was out, he didn't want her knocking on the door. The third time she did it, he called the front desk and the manager disciplined the maid. He told Travis the story and Travis told me but Dave didn't know I knew. As we drove away from the motel heading to the next show, I made up a story about how I heard the manager firing the maid. I said she was pleading for her job because she was a single mom with three kids and she wouldn't be able to pay her rent or feed the kids. Dave was silent, but Travis spoke up and asked, "Was that the maid you got fired Dave?" Dave didn't know what to say, but as I continued to embellish the story, he caught on that it was all a joke. We never admitted it was a joke and as we continued down the road, we would say things like, "I guess that maid's kids are trying to find something to eat."

A few weeks later Travis and I went to visit Dave in his room, and Travis spotted a spray bottle of cologne in the bathroom. Dave was laying on the bed and we were standing beside his open closet talking about something. Travis went to the bath-room and when he came out, he had that bottle of spray cologne and as we stood by the closet talking, Travis was spraying Dave's show jacket with cologne. When we finished talking, he quickly put the cologne back and we left. That night at the show, you could smell Dave coming about a mile away. Again, not wanting us to know it bothered him, he never said a word about it.

I can't imagine having this much fun doing a 9 to 5 job. Sure, the travel was rough, but the experiences we had made it worth it. I used to always say I got paid to travel and set up equipment and I played for free.

I owe Travis so much and I can never re-pay his kindness. Most everything I have today is because of him. His generosity and kind heart and soul are only part of this great man. We have rarely had an argument even though we've both had disagree-ments. I think the honesty and integrity we both have has made us a good team and I hope we continue on this path.

PHOTO BY BROOKE AUGUSTSSON

CHAPTER 42: COVID - THE MUSIC STOPPED

The year 2020 and COVID-19 brought an abrupt stop to live music. It was like something from a movie. It not only affected the entertainers, but it upset the entire entertainment industry. Agents, managers, venues, roadies, sound crews and companies, lighting crews and companies, tour bus operators and I could go on. It was a devastating blow.

For Travis and me, 2020 started normally with one of our biggest shows of the year at Riverwind Casino in Norman, Oklahoma. We played a show the first Saturday in January, commemorating Elvis Presley's birthday for a lot of years. Our crowds were always great and a line wrapped around the casino after the show to get a photo or autograph. In fact, the line after the show typically lasted longer than the show itself. Travis always brought in around 1,000 people each year. I should have gotten an inkling of what 2020 might bring when Riverwind decided to break the tradition and not invite us back for 2021. I never understood their reasoning since the fans had come to expect us to be there year after year and they continued to come. Sometimes I question corporate decision makers' reasoning, but this is one decision I never figured out.

Because Elvis's birthday was January 8, our schedule for that month was normally good. We felt blessed because January is ordinarily a slow month for entertainers. The Elvis tribute shows always did well in January and, in August, the month Elvis died. In 2020, we played the Hard Rock Casino near Tulsa, Oklahoma, and the Cherokee Casino in West Siloam Springs, Oklahoma. These venues normally booked us every year in January. We also played a new venue for us — the Blackbird Bend Casino in Onawa, Iowa.

In February, we played a couple of casinos in North Dakota and South Dakota. Our final live shows before the pandemic were in Hopkinsville, Kentucky, and Paris, Tennessee.

Travis and I did cruises in January, February and March and then it happened. We had been hearing about the virus the week before we got on board Royal Caribbean's "Vision Of The Seas." We were concerned about the virus because in the past, we had seen instances of the Norovirus break out and how quickly it would spread on the ships. Within a few days of an outbreak, lots of guests would be sick. There were "puke bags" everywhere you looked and you could smell that distinct odor. It wasn't a pleasant experience, even if you weren't sick. We would stay in our rooms if there was a Norovirus outbreak, other than to eat and do the shows. Luckily, Travis and I never got sick.

As the concern increased and the media started to focus on the virus, Charmaine loaded my suitcase with Clorox wipes and hand sanitizer. I was concerned, but at the time we boarded, we felt it would be safe to take the cruise. Masks had never been mentioned before, so everybody was walking around without that protection. At the time we thought it was just another virus where you'd be sick a few days and recover.

We boarded the ship and I saw an increased level of awareness and cleaning. The crew always did an excellent job of sanitizing the ship, but this time if you touched something it seemed there was someone there wiping that spot. If anyone had been diagnosed with symptoms of a virus, they would be quarantined and everything on the ship got wiped down from top to bottom. After each of our shows a crew would wipe every seat, door and hand railing in the house.

After we boarded, I went to my state room and turned on the TV. It seemed like each hour brought more dramatic and scary news about this new virus. Rumors spread about it being man made and released by the Chinese. Then came estimates of the death toll and how much more deadly it was going to be than the others. The word "pandemic" became the topic of a lot of conversations. This was an unusually short cruise for us, running from March 9 to March 13. Typically, we would be onboard for 7-10 days. In the four days we were on the ship, our thinking totally changed from not very concerned to being very anxious to get off this "Petri dish" and get back home.

Our fears elevated when the countries started denying us entry to their ports. Our time went like this. We flew to Grenada on March 9, spent the night and boarded the ship on March 10. By the time we boarded, we knew COVID was becoming a serious matter because of the screening we got before we boarded. They usually asked you typical health questions, but there were more questions and a temperature check. The level of cleaning was also accelerated and you could overhear passengers discussing the situation. We left Grenada on the night of March 10, headed for the island of Dominica. But when we got there on March 11, they denied us entry. We headed to our next destination of St. Maarten, arriving on March 12 only to be denied entry to that port. We knew it was getting serious and we were worried.

On March 13, 2020, the ship was allowed to dock in St. Thomas, Virgin Islands (a U.S. Territory). We had completed our shows and were anxious to get on a plane and get home as soon as possible. Getting off the ship was not an issue, but we expected extensive screenings at the airport and we were worried we may not be able to fly. When we arrived at the airport, everything was business as usual, and there were no screening or temperature checks. We felt like we had dodged one bullet getting off the ship, but now we had to get on a crowded plane where there were no masks or screening of the passengers. We flew to Miami, where we had to catch other flights to our homes. Again, there was no screening or temperature checks getting into the airport in Miami or for boarding our final flight home. They had no restrictions on travel at that point.

Once I landed in Nashville, there was a sigh of relief, but also some worry that I had been exposed either on the ship or on the planes. When I got home, I went into isolation and fortunately neither Travis nor I contracted the virus.

The impact of the virus on the entertainment industry was immediate. I got calls and emails nearly every day with the bad news of show cancellations and postponements. At that point, it looked like it we weren't going to be able to work for three months or so. Those three months turned into six months, then nine months. And, as of this writing, we are still unsure of the future.

On a side note, one of our friends, comedian Michele Balan was on a ship that was quarantined and she didn't get home for two months. After hearing her story, I was thankful for a safe and uneventful return for Travis and me.

As for the future of entertainment it will surely impact people and businesses going forward. Small venues are struggling or closing. All businesses associated with the music industry are struggling or closing. And worst of all is seeing my musician friends struggling to survive. Most musicians live week to week. When you completely shut off their income, it is devastating. If a good musician lost a job, he or she could normally find another job playing. In this case, there are no other gigs.

CHAPTER 43: MY NEAR-DEATH EXPERIENCES

As we travel through life, there are going to be dark times. I have miraculously survived several near-death experiences. I have often asked myself, "Why am I still here?" and after you read these stories maybe you'll understand my faith in God and why I believe He is watching over me. I have said many times that if I died tomorrow, I would die happy. I've had a wonderful life and done so many things people only dream about. I leave my fate in the hands of God and I often ask Him to lead me and I will follow.

On Monday, December 16, 1991, I had my first near-death experience. My fiancé, Tonya George, wanted to drive to her Mother's house to work on plans for our wedding, which was a few weeks away. I had a long day in the office and I was tired and wanted to go home. I finally gave in and we headed to the car, which was parked behind my office on Music Row. As I was getting in the car, I saw some coins laying in the parking lot beside the car. I hesitated, because I had two car accidents earlier in my life, and ironically, before each accident I had picked up coins in the parking lot. I convinced myself the other times were a fluke, so I picked up the coins and put them in my pocket.

It was early December and it was nearly dark. There was a cold mist hanging in the air and visibility was slightly limited. We were southbound on I-65 South near Exit 71 in Brentwood, Tennessee. I didn't see anything, I didn't hear anything but I felt the impact and was knocked off the interstate about 200 feet down by a fence line.

A drunk driver who was Northbound on I-65 had missed the turn and went down through the median and up into our lane of traffic on the Southbound side. He was airborne when he hit us. He was driving a Jeep Comanche pickup truck with a huge steel push bar on the front. He hit us broadside in my door. The impact was so great it pushed my intestines up through my diaphragm and into my chest cavity. It punctured my left lung, broke my ribs on the left side, ruptured my spleen and I could barely breathe. There was a lot of traffic during that time of day and within minutes people were coming to help me. One of those people was a male paramedic, who jumped in the car and talked to me the entire time. My fiancé was not seriously hurt and got out of the car where people tended to her injuries.

I was conscious through this entire ordeal. The pain was incredible. Up to that point in my life, I had questioned God. I would say, "If you're real show me something, give me a sign." I was expecting maybe something that would be a manifestation of His existence. As time passed and I'm in this car, I'm thinking about my two sons, Richard and Robert. Please let me get through this. If you're a believer, then this may not surprise you but I heard a voice that said, "I'm going to get you through this, but this is your sign." I'd always heard, "be careful what you wish for," but I never expected that to apply in a situation like this. Needless to say, I never questioned God after that moment.

I was in the car for a long time after the accident, and with my experience as an ambulance driver, I knew I was badly injured and that I was probably bleeding internally. I knew time was critical in getting me to the hospital. Firemen were cutting me out of the car as a Life Flight helicopter from Vanderbilt University Medical Center landed to get me to surgery.

I remained conscious, but the pain was getting more and more unbearable. I fully expected to lose consciousness or to die. I vaguely remember the helicopter ride. Everything was a blur. I remember being wheeled into surgery with a team of doctors, nurses and staff all around me. Orders were being shouted and as soon as I landed on the operating table, a doctor stuck a scalpel in my side and inserted a tube. The pain was unbearable and I jerked away. The doctor said, "You need to hold still" and I replied, "You're killing me." He replied, "No, we're trying to save your life, so hold still." That statement brought things into perspective and I settled down. Seconds later, I was out from the anesthesia.

Surgery lasted more than five hours as they put my intestines back in my gut and away from my heart and lungs, removed my spleen, removed part of my colon and sewed my diaphragm back in place. I woke up a couple of days later on a ventilator, with a row of staples running from my sternum to my bladder. I was a mess, but they had me on a morphine pump to keep me sedated and pain free. As soon as I was able, they allowed me administer a controlled dose when I needed it.

Every morning, noon and night the doctors would bring medical students in to visit me and discuss my injuries as a part of their training. I heard the words "lucky", "non-smoker" and "non-drinker" a lot. There was another person in ICU who was a smoker and drinker who wasn't doing as well as me. They were telling the students that the big difference was I had made better life choices.

I have always been allergic to wool and the blanket they had me laying on was wool. That and the morphine was making me itch. It was making my back and legs itch like crazy, but because of the ventilator I couldn't communicate that to the nurses, so I was miserable. There was a male nurse who was taking care of me on the midnight shift and he somehow figured out what was going on. The first thing he did was raise my legs up and scratch them for me. I was obviously ecstatic, so he would do that often and he found a blanket that wouldn't make me itch as much. It was a medical breakthrough, in my mind.

I was in the hospital for eight days and when I went home, I was bedridden for another 6 weeks. I remember one day I decided I wanted to get out of the house. I made my way to the car, struggled to get in and realized I needed to be back in bed. I decided I would let nature take its course and heal me before I tried that again.

On November 30, 2005, I had my second life-threatening experience. I was rearranging some things in my studio and I was hanging a picture high up on the wall and I had to stretch to reach to get picture high enough to hang. Shortly after that, my back started hurting really bad, but I had some people coming to the studio to record so I worked through the pain. As soon as they left I called out to my son Robert and told him about my back and I needed to go to the emergency room. I drove to the hospital and when I got to the emergency entrance I got out and went inside. Robert came around to the driver's side and jumped in to park the car.

As I entered the emergency room, I realized that I was confused. I wasn't at the emergency room entrance, but another part of the hospital. I turned around and Robert saw me and picked me up and took me to the right entrance. I was sweating profusely and when Robert looked at me, he asked if I was alright. The last thing I remember was saying, "I think I'm going to pass out."

Not only did I pass out, I was having a heart attack. Robert ran in the emergency room and got some help. By the time they got to me, I was blue and not getting any oxygen to my brain. Technically, I was dead. The E.R. staff ran to the parking lot and resuscitated me and it so happened one of the top cardiologists, Dr. Tracy Callister, was on duty.

After three days in an induced coma, I regained consciousness and I couldn't believe that I had a heart attack. I didn't smoke, I didn't drink and thought I was pretty active. I realized my downfall was eating at Wendy's nearly every day. I had a piece of plaque attached to my artery and it broke loose and shut off blood flow to my heart. It was a heart attack known as the "widow maker." I started thinking about all the places in the world I had been and "what if" this had happened when I was on a plane, a bus, or in the van in the middle of nowhere. I would have been dead, but somehow, I had survived. Thirty days later I was onstage, but I guess I didn't remember my incident after the car wreck. I wasn't ready and I had to sit down to play the show. I had no stamina for some time, but I gradually recovered.

I changed my diet, because that's what you do when you nearly die. I was dead for a few minutes, but I must confess I did not see the light. I did have the feeling after a few days that wherever it was that I went, I didn't want to come back to this world. I learned from that experience that whatever happens after you die must be so wonderful and peaceful that you don't want to come back.

At the end of November 2012, I woke up and started making the bed. I noticed spots in my vision and, at the same time, I realized my little finger and ring finger on my right hand were going numb. My wife, Charmaine, was at work and my son Robert was in his bedroom. I went to Robert's bedroom and the only thing I could say was, "We gotta go, we gotta go." He was confused as to why I was acting funny and called 911. I managed to get dressed and he helped me downstairs to the couch. I laid there waiting for the ambulance and paramedics.

Once they arrived, they started asking me questions. I heard them ask my son if I was on drugs. It was the strangest thing since they would ask me a question and I would answer them. But, according to my son, I was just talking gibberish and not giving them logical answers. In my mind, I was answering them perfectly.

They finally determined I was having a stroke and loaded me up and took me to the hospital where Charmaine was working. My son had called her and told her what was going on. Since she was working in the emergency room, she had them prepared for my arrival.

When I arrived, they immediately put me on the blood thinning drug Heperin and started questioning me again. At first my answers were the same gibberish I was giving the paramedics. As the medicine started working, I became more cognizant and able to communicate. After a few hours, I had no side effects from what happened and they sent me home.

This incident happened because I changed cardiologists and the new cardiologist took me off blood thinners. What he didn't realize was that due to my heart attack, a portion of my heart was not functioning and without blood thinners, blood would collect in that part of my heart and clot. A tiny portion of that clot broke loose and went to my brain.

I fully recovered from the stroke, leaving no side effects. I guess the scariest thing about having a stroke was the thought that I wouldn't be able to play music again. I think it's hard to imagine that in the life of any musician.

I dodged another bullet in 2018 when I was diagnosed with prostate cancer. Luckily, I had kept a close watch on my Prostate Specific Antigen (PSA) tests and as my number climbed out of the normal 2.6 to 4 range to a 7 my urologist suggested we do a biopsy that came back positive for cancer.

I was given three options for treatment. Radiation over a three-week period, radiation seed implantation and removal of the prostate. Removing the prostate was what I wanted to do, but because I would have to come off my blood thinner, the urologist suggested we stay away from that option. I agreed. The possibility of having another stroke was not an option. Radiation treatment over three weeks would have meant I couldn't work. For me, that was not an option. So, I opted for the radiation seed implants, which would be an outpatient procedure and get me back on the road.

I had the procedure on November 21, 2018, and I was working in the studio on November 28, 2018, and sailed out on a cruise ship, working with Travis on December 10, 2018.

With radiation seed implants, there is a risk to children and pregnant women for three months after the procedure. That meant if I was flying and I was seated near a woman or child, I had to inform them of my situation. I scared off quite a few women and kids over the next few months.

Another issue I had was the cruise ship port in Fort Lauderdale, Florida. When the cruise ship docks, you have to go through TSA to leave the ship. The TSA officers wear a device that vibrates if it detects radiation. When that device goes off, they quietly escort you to a private area for additional screening. The first time it happened, I wasn't sure what was happening and they didn't tell me. I knew if they took you to that private area it usually wasn't good, so I was quite concerned as to why that happened. I had a letter from my urologist stating I had radiation seeds implanted and typically that was enough to get me through security. But on two occasions, I was taken to the back room and tested with a Geiger Counter to ensure I wasn't carrying radioactive materials into the U.S.

On June 9, 2020, I suffered my second heart issue in the form of atrial fibrillation. The night of June 8, 2020, I had a pain in my stomach and I started to get sick. I was heaving and occasionally threw up some mucus in my throat from sinus drainage. Once I settled down, I went to bed hoping it would pass. At about 2 a.m. on June 9, 2020, I began another series of heaves and one particular heave was extremely strong. Following that extreme heave, I began to have chest pains like I had never experienced before and that pain radiated a short distance down my left arm. I woke Charmaine and told her we needed to go to the hospital.

Once we arrived at the emergency room, I got out and walked inside. Charmaine was not allowed to come with me, due to COVID restrictions, and went back to the car to wait. Once I told them I was having chest pains, they sent a wheelchair to take me back to the E.R. I told them I would walk and I did.

When I reached the exam room and laid down, the doctor came in and started asking me questions. At that time, I could feel myself going faint and I told them I thought I was going to pass out.

Not only did I pass out, but I went into tachycardia, which meant my heart was beating too fast and erratically. They had to use the defibrillator paddles to bring me back. A few minutes after I regained consciousness, I had the second episode of passing out and again they shocked me back to life. I had five episodes, where they had to use the defibrillator. That, along with the medicines they were giving to stabilize my heart rhythm, brought me to a stable condition.

I don't remember much, but this time I distinctly remember seeing that bright light so many people have described in near death experiences after passing out the fourth time. I didn't experience anything like this during my first heart attack, so I was skeptical that it happens. I can tell you this time it was very real and peaceful. It was so bright I can't even describe it. It was in the center of a garden-looking area and it looked much like the sun would shine low on the horizon just above some vegetation. I had that same peaceful experience with my first heart attack, so it was like this just cemented my belief in God and Heaven even more.

After 11 days in the hospital and a defibrillator implant, I went home about as weak as you can imagine. I could only walk a few steps at a time and it was taking a while to recover from that incident.

Following the heart attack on June 9, 2020, I didn't feel like I was recovering as fast as I should, but everybody kept telling me to give myself time to heal. Come to find out I had Ecoli. It was another setback, and due to my prostate issues. My prostate had swollen and was cutting off my urine flow. That urine collected in my bladder and Ecoli developed and I became septic. On the night of August 9, 2020, I knew I wasn't feeling up to par but I thought it might be my slow recovery from the heart attack. I was starting to chill and Charmaine got me an extra blanket. I was shaking uncontrollably and I knew this was more than a simple chill. So, off to the hospital, where they discovered the Ecoli had spread to my bloodstream and I was on the verge of septic shock. The next few days in the hospital were rough. It took four days in the hospital for them to get me stabilized. I was extremely weak and stayed in bed for another week or so. I'm beginning to wonder when this will all end. It's been a year of COVID 19 and all the health problems I could handle and I prayed it would soon be over and I could enjoy life again.

CHAPTER 44: MY BIG REGRET

Writing this book has been a remarkable experience. I have relived the fun times, the sad times and even rediscovered my shortcomings and things I regret. I have been married three times and each wife sacrificed a lot for me. A lot of nights at home alone, a lot of attending events alone - school plays, birthdays, holidays, awards ceremonies, graduations, ball games, funerals and other events. These are things you can't fix because they only happen once. I'm sure I disappointed a lot of people but I especially want to apologize to the ex-wives, my current wife and children. They tell you the music business requires sacrifice and this is one of those sacrifices that most musicians hate. I've since thought about what my loved ones must have been doing and going through while I was traveling and living this dream. My dream had to be their nightmare and yet they stood by me.

My first wife, Judi was a jewel. We met in Junior High School and were married when I was 19 and she was 17. I was consumed by music but she stood by me. She practically raised our two sons, Richard and Robert, on her own. She was there alone when I should have been there. At the time, I convinced myself it was OK for me to be away and I would be there the next time or we could make up for lost time later. Judi reached her breaking point and we divorced in the mid 80s.

My second wife Tonya was much like Judi. We had three children, Chrysten, Courtney and Ryan. She stood by me and, she too, attended most of the family events alone. We both grew apart and our relationship ended in divorce in the early 2000s. With two failed marriages I should have looked more at myself as the culprit but I didn't. Again, I traveled and played music at every opportunity not considering the damage I may be doing to my family.

My third and current wife Charmaine has been there as well. After meeting her and her husband in Scotland, I could tell she wasn't happy. We maintained contact after the show and shortly after she decided to get a divorce. She came to visit in late 2006 and didn't go back.

She has attended events on my behalf or for my children and grandchildren when I couldn't be there. She even represented my at funerals of friends. Age has been a great eye-opener and hopefully I can be there for all of them in the future.

All my children are grown now, they've all turned out great in spite of my shortcomings. A testament to their mothers. We have a good relationship, still, I regret missing out on all those special times and events. While I don't feel like I deserve it, I hope they have forgiven me.

CHAPTER 45: IN CONCLUSION

A s I look back on my life, I realize how blessed I have been. I've done a lot of things that people only dream of and it all started with me having a dream. I left West Virginia not knowing if I would be successful or not, but I had to try. My feeling was if I tried and failed, at least I tried. So, if you have a dream, you owe it to yourself to try and achieve it. I'm living proof it is possible.

What's ahead for me? I hope to continue to be involved in things I love. Music is first and foremost and while my road days are coming to an end, you may see me in a Nashville club filling in for someone. I'll continue to handle business for Travis LeDoyt, do publicity and promotional work and be heavily involved in recording projects with both new and established clients. I'm also continuing my interest in photography, fishing and flying my drones.

No matter what the future holds, I just ask God to lead the way. I've told people that death does not scare me. I have been so fortunate that if I died tomorrow, I couldn't complain.

I have a lot left to share with musicians, singers and creative people in general. It requires work and effort and that's where many creative people fail. They get their reward from performing and not at the bank. It's hard to navigate the very tough business side of the music business. My secret of success has been to learn the business side of the business - not just the creative side. That was the result of learning early in my career what it takes to be successful.

I hope you have enjoyed the book and all the stories. There are literally hundreds of stories and people in my life that I couldn't include in this book due to constraints. That does not diminish my love for all of you. That includes anyone who has been a part of my life. Thank you for reading and hopefully we will see you somewhere down the road.

MY FAMILY

SON ROBERT

SON RYAN

SON RICHARD

DAUGHTER IN LAW JENNIFER

GRANDDAUGHTER SARAH

GRANDSON SEAN

DAUGHTER COURTNEY

DAUGHTER CHRYSTEN

CHARMAINE MCVEY

TIM MCGRAW

JOHNNY WRIGHT   KITTY WELLS

JOHNNY PAYCHECK

SAM MOORE
SAM & DAVE

MAUREEN MCCORMICK
"MARSHA BRADY"

ACKNOWLEGMENTS

I wanted to include many more friends and stories but, as you may imagine, there were too many people and too many stories to include them all. I want you to know how much all of you mean to me.

Thanks to God for allowing me to continue to live and work in a business I love and to Pastor Jimmy Ford for his wonderful messages.

To all my family members, both immediate and extended for making the good times better. I also appreciate all the help and support along the way.

To all the loyal fans and my studio clients, who have provided the money that pays the bills. Special thanks to all the talent buyers, booking agents and venues who continue to hire my acts.

To my musician family for all the great times on the road, on stage and in the recording studio. It is truly a family.

To all my West Virginia friends, especially my classmates over the years and the people who worked with me in the funeral business or coal mines.

To all the many friends I have made over the years. Thanks for the memories.

Dick McVey   www.dickmcvey.com